1234 Wacky, Witty and Wonderful Words

by

Paul Sloane and Des MacHale

Published by Athehta Systems, printed by Amazon.

A portion of the royalties from this book will go to the charity Step by Step, headquartered in Aldershot, which supports disadvantaged young people.

ISBN 9798594861961

Contents

Preface

Words are precious and powerful things. They are the tools we use to communicate our ideas. This book is a collection of our favourite fascinating words. It includes cunning curiosities, remarkable rarities, wonderful words and tremendous trivia. All the words are in use or have been in use in the English language. Most of the entries are serious and informative but occasionally we have sprinkled in something unexpected and facetious (a word which has all five vowels in alphabetical order). We trust the reader will spot these surprises and forgive us for their inclusion. We have shown the wacky, witty and wonderful words in capitals and the foreign root words in italics. We have not shown etymology for every word but only for those where we find it interesting. The book should appeal to logophiles (a word of Greek origin) and cruciverbalists (a word of Latin origin.) How did we choose the words to include? The answer is unscientifically. We simply chose the words that we found curious, beautiful, fascinating or remarkable. Words like halcyon, mountweazel, procrustean, tawdry, synecdoche and mangelwurzel. The book is not designed to be read from start to finish. Instead, please dip into it whenever you feel the need for some verbal inspiration. If you have any comments, suggestions or additions for the book please let us know.

Acknowledgements

With sincere thanks to the following people who contributed funds and words in the launch campaign.

Ajaz Ahmed, Aliskha Cooper, Andy Green, Ann Sloane, Anne MacHale, Arthur Morton Jack, Bob Critchlow, Bruno Woeran, Chris Sivewright, Chris Turnbull, David Adams, David Arundale, David Schnepper, Denver Dias, Derek Arden, Derek Overton, Duncan Robertson, Frank Morton Jack, Gordon Tredgold, Graham Churchill, Hannah Sloane, Howard Ford, Jackie Phelps, James Sloane, Bill Penn, Farouk Massouh, John Holroyd, Jenny Jackson, Jerome Phelps, Joe Burnie, John Allen, John Carpenter, John Devlin, John Wallis, Jonathan Gold, Madeleine Phelps, Mark Durrant, Michael Annett, Mike Roycroft, Nichola Goom, Nigel Bleach, Norman Spence, Pat Hartwell, Peter Bonsall, Peter Cinelli, Richard Snook, Rick Squires, Robin Perry, Roger Jeynes, Russell James, Steve Pearce, Toby Phelps, Valentina Morton Jack, William Morton Jack, Yvonne Cohen.

With thanks to the following photographers on Pixabay.com: Alligator by Jeff Leonhardt, Axolotl by Tinwe, Bustard by Michelle Maria, Florence Cathedral by Andrea Spallanzani, Everest by Simon Steinberger, Geysir by Sharon Ang, Librocubicularist by Amberrose Nelson, Ombrifuge by Freephotos, Samovar by Dmitry Demidov, Thaler by Volker-76, Uzi by Shutterbug75, Windsor Castle by Roman Grac, Zonkey by Dorte Tang

My lad chewed and swallowed a dictionary. We gave him Epsom salts - but we can't get a word out of him.

Les Dawson

The Words

AA a word from the Hawaiian, meaning a volcanic rock. The first word after A in most dictionaries.

AARDVARKS would have been the first entrants in the ark if Noah had admitted animals in alphabetical order. Aardvark is Dutch for earth pig.

ABBREVIATION has 12 letters and 5 syllables. Because it is such a long word abb is sometimes used as an abbreviation of abbreviation.

ABECEDARIAN means pertaining to the alphabet and ABC, rudimentary. As a noun it means a beginner, a learner or an elementary teacher.

ABOMINABLE an explosive device inside a male of the cattle family.

ABRACADABRA has only one vowel used five times. It means a spell or conjuring word. It appeared in a 2nd century poem by the Roman savant and poet, Serenus Sammonicus, who was murdered at a banquet in 212 on the orders of the Emperor Caracalla.

ABSCONDED went off with the first five letters of the alphabet in order.

ABSINTHE a drink which makes the heart grow fonder.

ABSQUATULATE a rare word meaning to abscond or leave hurriedly. It may be based on a mock-Latin negation of squat. Another American neologism for this action is SKEDADDLE.

ABSTEMIOUS and FACETIOUS have all five vowels in order. If you consider Y to be a vowel then you can add abstemiously and facetiously.

ACADEMY from the Greek *Akadēmía*, the name of the gymnasium near Athens where Plato taught, from *Akademos*, a hero of the Trojan War.

ACOUSTIC something you play pool with.

ADAM'S APPLE Adam was the first man in Hebrew
mythology reputedly driven out of the Garden of Eden
by God for eating an apple given to him by his wife Eve.
The cartilaginous projection (the thyroid) prominent in
the male throat, is supposed to be where the apple stuck
as he ate it. But according to Mark Twain, it was there to
keep the hangman's rope in place.

ADOBE an unfired brick made from clay and dried in the
sun. A structure made of adobe bricks. From the Arabic
al-tob the brick.

ADULTERY the word has nothing to do with ADULT. It
comes from adulterate - to corrupt or contaminate.

AEGILOPS is a genus of plants generally known as goat
grasses. AEGILOPS is also the longest word with all of its
letters in alphabetical order with no letter repeated.

AFGHANISTAN contains the letters FGH consecutively.

AFTERMATH a consequence. The word is a corruption of *aftermowth*, an old word meaning a second growth of grass that grows after the first mowing of the year.

AGELAST someone who never laughs. From the Greek *agelastos*, grave or gloomy.

AGNOSTIC a person who is unsure whether there is a God or not. A word coined by the British anthropologist Thomas Huxley from the Greek *agnostos* unknown.

AIBOHOPHOBIA is a PALINDROME which means fear of palindromes. It was deliberately constructed by combining the suffix -phobia with its reverse.

AIDS an acronym for Acquired Immunodeficiency Syndrome.

ALAN SMITHEE is a standard pseudonym that filmmakers put in the credits when they do not want their real name to be known, because the film is a total turkey.

ALASKA is the only US State whose name can be spelled out using only one line of the keyboard. Alaska is the

14

most northerly, most westerly, and most easterly state (because part of it lies across the International Date Line) of the USA. Hawaii is the most southerly.

ALCHEMISTS sought to use ALCHEMY (an Arabic word) to turn base metals like lead into gold. Later scientists scoffed at this idea, but it now can be done using nuclear physics. The irony is that the process is more expensive than the gold is worth. If it could be done cheaply, gold would become so common that it would lose its value. (See CHEMISTRY)

ALCOHOL comes from the Arabic, *Al Kohl*, meaning the powder used to stain eyelids. This was an extract and the word alcohol originally meant the essential extract or essence of something. Wine-alcohol was the term used to describe the essence of wine which made you intoxicated. This was abbreviated to alcohol. Incidentally, alcohol does not make you fat; it makes you lean.

ALEATORY depending on chance or a gamble. From the Latin *alea*, a die or DICE.

ALGEBRA a central branch of mathematics. It comes from Arabic words *al jabr,* meaning the reunion of broken parts.

ALIBI a proof that you were somewhere else when something happened (often a crime). From the Latin *alibi*, elsewhere.

ALICE is an anagram of another girl's name, CELIA. And DOROTHEA is a rearrangement of THEODORA.

Alligator

ALLIGATOR from the Spanish *el lagarto,* the lizard. When the judge asked, 'Who is making these allegations?' the plaintiff replied, 'Your honour, I am the alligator'.

ALLIUMPHOBE a person who hates garlic.

ALLOCATE is what you say when you meet Kate.

ALLOPATHY medical treatment of a condition with substances that have the opposite effect as the symptoms e.g. applying an icepack to alleviate sunburn. Allopathy is science-based and is the opposite of HOMOEOPATHY in which tiny portions of a substance that causes symptoms of a disease are used to treat the disease.

ALLYCUMPOOSTER satisfactory and all correct. One of the few words of Cornish origin to have made it into English. Others are BAMFOOZLE, to deceive by trickery, KIDDLYWINK, an unlicenced beer shop or SHEBEEN, and GRAMMERSOW, a woodlouse.

ALMONER an old name for a social worker; originally a distributor of alms to the poor.

ALOFT *loft* is the Old Norse word for the sky or heaven while *á* means on. So bearing someone aloft means carrying them up to heaven.

ALOPECIA premature and complete baldness in men. From the Greek *alopek*, a fox, because the condition resembles mange in foxes.

ALTOGETHER in the altogether means completely naked, a word introduced by George DuMaurier in his 1894 novel Trilby.

ALPHABET has just three syllables yet contains 26 letters. The word alphabet comes from *alpha beta*, the first two words in the Greek alphabet. Among the shorter alphabets are Hawaiian with just 12 letters, Irish Gaelic with 18 and Italian with 21. Sanskrit has 49 letters and Cambodian has a massive 74.

AMANUENSIS a literary clerk who writes from dictation. From the Latin *servus a manu*, meaning a slave at hand.

AMATEUR someone who practises something for the love of it. The word comes from the Latin *amare*, to love, which is also the source of amiable, amorous and paramour.

AMAZON the world's greatest river in volume of water and the world's greatest online retailer in volume of sales. But in Greek mythology Amazons were warrior women from Scythia. They were reputed to cut off their right breasts to enable them to draw bowstrings more effectively. Some believe the river took its name from these women because Spanish explorers in Brazil in 1540 thought they saw female warriors there.

AMBIDEXTROUS literally means right-handed on both sides, from the Latin *ambi* both and *dexter* right-handed. Its opposite is the rare word, AMBILEVOUS, literally left-handed on both sides, meaning clumsy.

AMEN is a Hebrew word meaning 'so be it'. We sing a-men and not a-women at the end of a hymn because it is a hymn and not a her.

AMERICA is named after the Italian navigator Amerigo Vespucci (1454-1512) who made two trips exploring the New World and claimed to have discovered it. He put forward the idea that it was a new continent, and he was the first to call it Novus Mundus 'New World.' See VENEZUELA.

AMETHYST a form of quartz crystal with a beautiful purple colour due to the presence of iron oxide. Roman women believed that if they wore an amethyst amulet, then their husbands would remain faithful to them. The stone was used in Bishops' rings. The name comes from Greek words meaning 'without drunkenness' based on the (mistaken!) belief that if you wore an amethyst pendant or drank from a goblet made from amethyst, you could not get drunk, no matter how much wine you consumed. Try telling that to the judge!

AMOK as used in the expression to run amok. The word comes from a Malay word *amuck* meaning to attack furiously.

AMMONIA a colourless gas with a strong pungent smell. It gets its name from the Ancient Egyptian god Amun (changed to Ammon by the Greeks). Worshipers of Amun performed spiritual rites with ammonia in the god's honour. Ammonia is the main constituent of smelling salts which were often used for the revival of fainting Victorian heroines. Chemical formula NH3 which is also an opening move in chess.

AMPERSAND the symbol &. It is short for 'and.' It is a contraction of 'and per se and'.

AMPHIBIAN literally means having two forms of life. From the Greek *amphi* on both sides and *bios* life. Formerly used to describe any sort of animal at home on land and in the water, including crocodiles and beavers, but now restricted to animals like frogs and newts, that start their lives in water and mature on land. An amphibious vehicle is at home in water and on land.

ANACHRONISM a chronological mistake or discrepancy, such as a painting of Julius Caesar wearing a watch. A film had a scene where a general addressed his troops, 'Men of the Middle Ages, you are about to embark on the Hundred Years War'. From the Greek *ana,* wrong, and *khronos*, time.

ANDANTE a musical instruction indicating that a piece is to be played fairly slowly, literally at walking speed. It is the present participle of the Italian verb *andare*, to walk.

ANECDOTAGE a state where somebody repeatedly tells stories over and over again to the same audience. This is a PORTMANTEAU word (see entry) of anecdote and dotage.

ANGERED is an anagram of ENRAGED.

ANTEPENULTIMATE the last but two. Penultimate is next to last and antepenultimate is one before that. From the Latin *ante* before, *paene* almost and *ultimus* last.

ANORAK comes to us from the Innuits in Greenland. It meant a coat or jacket but now it can also mean a geeky nerd who wears such a thing.

ANOSMIA is the loss of the sense of smell.

ANTANACLASIS is when a word or phrase is repeated, but in different senses. From the Greek, *antanaklasis*, meaning reflection. E.g. The American football coach Vince Lombardi said to his team: 'If you aren't fired with enthusiasm, you will be fired, with enthusiasm'. See BUFFALO.

ANTEDILUVIAN very old, literally before Noah's flood. From the Latin *ante*, before and *diluvium*, a flood.

ANTELOPE an insect who runs away to get married.

ANTIPODES the diametrically opposite point from a given place on the earth. Often used as a synonym for Australia and New Zealand, but the antipodes of most land locations lie in the oceans. The word was used in Plato's Dialogues with meaning 'with feet opposite ours'. Incidentally, the stress is on the 'tip', a trap for the unwary.

ANTONYM a word of opposite meaning to a given word. ANTONYM is the antonym of SYNONYM and a syonym of opposite.

APERITIF an opening drink taken as an appetizer. It is a French word derived from the Latin *aperire* to open. However, some people think that APERITIF is a set of dentures.

APOCHRYPHA certain old books never accepted by some Christian Churches as part of the canonical bible. So apocryphal means of dubious authority or spurious. From the Greek *apo* from and *kryptein* to hide.

APPLE is one of the oldest words in the English language. It is from Indo-European sources. Other very old words include BAD, GOLD, TOWN and TIN.

AQUABIB someone who drinks only water. Based on the Latin *aqua,* water and *bibere,* to drink. Very useful as the designated driver.

ARACHIBUTYROPHOBIA a fortunately very rare condition where people become hysterical when peanut butter sticks to the roof of their mouth.

ARCHAEOLOGIST somebody whose career is in ruins.

ARCHETYPICAL is the longest word with the most letters in their natural alphabetical position. A is in position 1, C in 3, E in 5, I in 9 and L in 12.

AREA is highly unusual in that it has only four letters but three syllables.

ARENA a sporting or entertainment venue. Arena is the Latin word for sand. Ancient amphitheatres were strewed with sand which helped soak up the blood from combats.

ARGON is a chemical element with atomic number 18. The name is derived from the Greek word *argon* meaning lazy or inactive, as a reference to the fact that the element undergoes almost no chemical reactions. Argon is the third most common gas in the air we breathe and comprises about 1% of the atmosphere.

ARGIE-BARGIE a British colloquialism for a wrangling argument or verbal dispute. It became a popular term for the Falklands War.

ARIZONA is the only US State to contain the letter Z. There is only one letter that does not appear in any State's name. It is Q.

ARNOLD is a boy's name which has two anagrams which are also boys' names – ROLAND and RONALD.

ASBESTOS a fire-proof but toxic mineral. It is a Greek word referring to a mythical stone which, once set alight, could never be extinguished.

ASPARAGUS a food plant of the lily family. Originally called 'sparrowgrass'. It has the curious property of making some people's urine smell odd.

ASSASSIN originally a member of a Shia Muslim sect sent out on a suicidal mission to murder enemies. It was believed that they were high on drugs and the word comes from the Arabic *hashshashin*, hash user.

ASSESSES is the longest word that uses only one consonant and the shortest word in which one letter appears five times.

ASSONANCE similar vowel sounds that correspond to alliteration for consonants. A good example is 'The rain in Spain falls mainly in the plain.'

ASTRONOMER is an anagram of MOON STARER.

ATARAXIA is tranquillity and freedom from anxiety.

ATROPHY something you win at sport.

ATTIRE The difference between a poorly dressed man on a unicycle and a well-dressed man on a bicycle.

AUGUST and POLISH both change their meanings when the first letter is capitalised.

AULOPHOBIA fear of flutes. From the Greek *aulos*, a flute.

AUNT SALLY originally a large doll at which things were thrown at a fair to win prizes. Nowadays, someone everyone is entitled to abuse and criticise. But nobody seems to know who the original Aunt Sally was.

AURORA AUSTRALIS dramatic light effects seen in the sky at high altitudes in the southern hemisphere. The southern cousin of the more famous Aurora Borealis.

AUSTRALIA means Southern Country. From Latin *Terra Australis*.

AUTODIDACT a person who is self-taught.

AVATAR initially meant the incarnation and descent of a deity in earthly form. It comes from the Sanskrit word *avatara*, meaning descent.

AVERAGE comes from the old French *avarie,* a derivative of an Arabic word meaning damaged merchandise. When a ship or its cargo was damaged at sea, the owners shared the expense, or average. An average then became any equal distribution or division.

AVIVA is a girl's name from the Hebrew meaning springlike or youthful. AVIVA is a PALINDROME and a mirror palindrome, identical with its reflected image. Other examples include AHA, OXO, MUM, and TOOT.

AVOCADO the name for this oily fruit comes from the Aztec language Nahuatl where it also meant a testicle.

AVOIDABLE is what a bullfighter tries to do.

AWFUL originally meant something awe-inspiring – either wonderful or terrible. Now it means bad or unpleasant. Similarly, AWFULLY is now a synonym for very. It is a victim of VERBICIDE.

AWKWARD clumsy, ungraceful, difficult to deal with. From the old Norse *afug* turning the wrong way. Awkward contains the rare three letter sequence WKW. The only other word which does is the plant HAWKWEED. The clumsy clinician Dr. Awkward is a PALINDROME.

AWOL if someone goes AWOL then they are Absent Without Official Leave.

AXIOM a self-evident truth, a fundamental and accepted principle. From the Greek *axioein* to take for granted.

AXOLOTL a Mexican salamander. A type of amphibian that looks like a walking fish. A wonderful Aztec word.

An Axolotl

B

BACCALAUREATE a bachelor's degree, is a twelve letter word in which all of the consonants are in alphabetical order.

BACTERIAL is an anagram of CALIBRATE.

BADMINTON a game played with a shuttlecock. British army officers brought the game home from India. Derived from Badminton House, the home of the Duke of Beaufort, where the game first was played in England. The house is also famous for equestrian events.

BAFFONA a woman with a not unpleasing slight moustache. A word of Italian origin.

BAGPIPES the missing link between noise and music.

BAILIWICK originally, a region under the jurisdiction of a bailiff. In old English *wic* meant a village. It has come to mean the area of responsibility over which an individual has control.

BAKSHEESH is a payment or bribe to expedite service. It is a Persian word meaning gift.

BALACLAVA is a Russian word of Tatar origin. A knitted hat that covers the face. First used in the British army during the Crimean war of 1853-56. From the name of the town of Balaklava, russified Tatar *Baliqlava*.

BALONEY nonsense; called after inferior sausage from Bologna in Italy.

BAMBOOZLE to trick, to confuse, to fool, to con. Origin uncertain but possibly from Scottish *bombaze*, to confound, or from the French *embabouiner* to make a fool (literally 'baboon') of.

BANANA is the only Wolof word in common use in English. Wolof is a language of Senegal, the Gambia and Mauritania, and the native language of the Wolof people.

BANANAS if you peel off the first letter you get another fruit, pineapple - ANANAS.

BANKRUPT means a broken bench. BANK comes from the Italian *banca*, bench because moneylenders would sit behind a bench. If the moneylender failed to meet his debts, then his bench was broken.

BANTING William Banting (1797--1878) was a seriously overweight London undertaker who had tried many diets to no avail. Finally, he decided to eliminate sugars and starches (i.e. carbohydrates) and consume large amounts of meat and fish (i.e protein). He lost a lot of weight and lived to a ripe old age. Dieting became known as 'banting'. Many years later, the very successful Atkins diet had many of the features of banting.

BANSHEE in Celtic folklore, a female spirit who wails in a distinctive manner foretelling a death often in a privileged family. From the Irish *bean si*, a fairy woman.

BARBADOS was named by Spanish explorers *los barbudos*, meaning the bearded ones. This was a reference to the bearded fig-trees indigenous to the island whose long hanging roots looked like beards.

BARBARIAN derived from the Greek word *bárbaros*, meaning babbler. It was used to describe people from non-Greek speaking countries such as Persia and Egypt, whose speech, to Greek ears, was unintelligible and sounded like 'bar,bar,bar'.

BARBECUE a line of people waiting outside a hairdressers. The verb meaning to grill on a gridiron comes from the Arawakan language used in Haiti.

BARBITURATES were invented by Dr. Von Baeyer, who called them after his girlfriend Barbara.

BARDOLATRY a word coined by George Bernard Shaw meaning excessive worship of Shakespeare.

BARN BURNER an exciting or dramatic event, especially a sports contest.

BEDLAM meaning a place of uproar or madness is a corruption of Bethlehem Royal Hospital, a psychiatric institute in London.

BEELINE Bees are believed to use the shortest possible path to reach sources of nectar; hence the expression 'to make a beeline'.

BEHEMOTH a biblical word for a large animal, believed to be a hippopotamus. Hence anything large and powerful.

BELGIAN a European, is an anagram of BENGALI, an Indian.

BELLADONNA deadly Nightshade contains a poisonous chemical said to have been used by Italian ladies to swell the pupils of their eyes and so appear even more beautiful. *Bella donna* is Italian for beautiful lady.

BERMUDA TRIANGLE was originally known as the Bermuda Quadrilateral, and then one day one side mysteriously went missing.

BERSERK to go berserk means to become frenziedly violent or destructive. The word comes from the Old Norse (or Viking) words *björn* bear and *serkur* shirt. *Berserkir* were
Norse warriors who worked themselves into a frenzy before battle.

BIBLIOKLEPT a fancy name for someone who steals books. From the Greek *biblio*, book and *kleptes*, thief.

BICAMERAL referring to a system of government having two legislative chambers, usually an upper house and a lower house. From the Latin *bi* two and *camera* room.

BIGOREXIA is a condition where someone wants to be bigger and more muscular, often by using steroids. It is the opposite of ANOREXIA.

BIGAMIST an Italian fog.

BIGOT a person who has blind or excessive zeal and is often dismissive of others. The word comes from an old English oath, By God.

BIKINI a woman's swimming costume in two brief parts. Bikini is the name of an atoll in the Marshall Islands where atom bomb experiments were carried out in the 1940s. The effect of the bikini on men was said to be similar to that of the bomb.

BILLABONG a detached loop of an Australian river, often one that dries up in summer. It features in the song Waltzing Matilda, the alternative Australian National Anthem. From the Aboriginal *billa* river and *bung* dead.

BIMBO a disparaging term for an attractive but stupid woman. From the Italian *bambino*, baby.

BIPOLAR a white bear who goes on holiday to Antarctica.

BIREME a galley having two banks of oars. From the Latin *bi*, two, and *remus*, an oar. There were also triremes (three banks) and even quinqueremes (five banks).

BIRO named after Laszlo Jozsef Biro, a Hungarian-Argentine inventor who patented the first commercially successful modern ballpoint pen. This was not just his pen name.

BISCUIT means cooked twice. From the French *bis* twice *cuit* cooked.

BISSEXTILE a fancy name for a leap year. Having an INTERCALARY day.

BITE the phrase 'bite the dust' comes from Homer's Iliad written in the 8th century BC.

BIZARRE is *bizarre* in French and *bizarro* in Spanish. It comes from the Basque *bizarra* meaning beard. The Basques were clean-shaven and thought that foreign men wearing beards looked decidedly odd – or bizarre.

BLACKBALL to reject a candidate for election for membership of a club, by placing a black ball in an urn as an adverse vote during a secret ballot.

BLACKMAILED is the longest word all of whose letters come from the first half of the alphabet.

BLOCKBUSTER a smash hit book or movie, a term originating in the United States. For a movie, it meant that the queue at the box office went all the way round the corner of the block.

BLOG a website containing personal observations and comments. First used in 1999. A contraction of web log.

BLUNDER comes from the Old Norse word *blundra* which means to shut your eyes and so to walk around banging into things.

BLURB a short piece of publicity or praise. A word coined by American writer and humourist Gelett Burgess in 1907.

BOBBY an English policeman was often called a BOBBY or a PEELER. Both names come from Sir Robert Peel, who was British Prime Minister and surely the only person to have something called after both his first and second names.

BOG comes from the Irish for soft.

BOONDOGGLE a wasteful and unnecessary undertaking. It became a contemptuous word in the USA in the 1930s for make-work projects for the unemployed when the latter were offered courses in how to make Scouts' braids knowns a boondoggles.

BOTULISM is a nasty form of food poisoning. It is derived from the Latin word for sausage *botulus* because it was originally traced to eating tainted sausages.

BOYCOTT to punish somebody by refusing to have anything to do with them either socially or commercially. Called after Captain Charles Boycott, a cruel land agent in the West of Ireland in the 19th Century on whom this treatment was very successful.

BOOKKEEPER is the only word with three consecutive sets of double letters.

BOOT when a computer BOOTS it loads a software program to get going. The original expression was that it pulls itself up by its own bootstraps.

BOOTLEGGER a maker of illicit whiskey who used to store his produce in his long boots. The word's popularity increased in the U.S. during Prohibition (1920-1933).

BLOOMERS are a form of women's underwear. They are named after Amelia Bloomer, a newspaper publisher who was a leading member of the Women's Rights movement.

BONFIRE a large fire in the open air, often to celebrate an important event. Originally a bone fire where bones were burned.

BOOK comes from the Old German word for beech, *bok*, because messages were carved into the soft pieces of beech wood. Latin and Sanskrit also have words for writing are based on tree names of birch and ash. And the French word for book, *livre*, comes from a Latin word for the tree bark.

BORBORYGMUS is an intestinal noise caused by moving gas – otherwise known as a tummy rumble. From the Greek borboryzein to rumble. The subject of this limerick.

I sat next the duchess at tea.

It was just as I feared it would be.

Her rumblings abdominal,

were simply phenomenal,

and everyone thought it was me!

BOWIE a knife with a large blade. Named after Colonel James Bowie who died at the Battle of the Alamo in 1836.

BRAINIAC a very smart person. A PORTMANTEAU word of brain and maniac. Brainiac appeared in 1956 as a super intelligent adversary of Superman in the Action Comics series.

BRAINWASHING an attempt to alter or control the thoughts and beliefs of another person against his will by psychological techniques. First used in 1950, a literal translation of Chinese *xi nao*. A term from the Korean War.

BRASS TACKS getting down to brass tacks means getting down to business. In old American drapery stores, there were two brass tacks positioned a yard apart on the counter for measuring cloth. When these were used, the customer was serious about purchasing some fabric.

BRATWURST the naughtiest child.

BRAZIL the country is named after the nut and not the other way round.

BREASTSUMMER (or BRESSUMMER) a term from architecture, meaning a beam across a broad opening, supporting a superstructure. Derived from the French *sommier*, a pack horse which could bear great weight.

BREN GUN a light automatic rifle name after the Czech town of Brno where it was originally invented, and Enfield in England where it was manufactured.

BRIDEZILLA a bride to be who becomes neurotically obsessed with every detail of her wedding.   A combination of bride and the monster Godzilla.

BRIMSTONE an old name for sulphur, believed to fuel the fires of Hell. It may be derived from the Dutch *barnsteen*, meaning amber.

BRITAIN comes from the Greek word *prittanoi* meaning the tattooed people.

BROWNIE POINTS have nothing to do with Girl Guides. The term comes from the brown-nosing tactics of underlings to curry favour with their bosses.

BUBBLE and SQUEAK bacon and cabbage first boiled together when they bubble, and then fried together when they squeak. A delicious traditional British dish.

BUCCANEER originally meant someone who cured flesh on a barbecue. Boucan is French for a barbecue used in the West Indies. Buccaneers are also known as pirates, privateers and freebooters.

BUCCULA is a medical name for a double chin.

BUCOLIC means pertaining the country or pastoral.
From the Greek *boukolikos* a herdsman. Not to be
confused with BUBONIC, a nasty type of plague.

BUDAPEST the city of Budapest, the capital of Hungary,
actually consists of twin cities on either side of the river
Danube, BUDA and PEST.

BUDGERIGAR a small parrot. It is the third most popular
pet in the world after dogs and cats. From the
Yuwaalaraay, an Australian aboriginal language of
northern New South Wales, *gijirrigaa,* meaning good
food. This was not because the aborigines ate them but
because if they followed the birds' migrations it would
lead to water and food.

BUENOS AIRES in Argentina means good winds. And
while we are in South America, MONTEVIDEO, Uruguay
means I see a mountain, LA PAZ, Bolivia means peace
and RIO DE JANEIRO, Brazil means January River (it was
discovered in January 1502).

BUFFALO has three different meanings: a town near
Niagara Falls, the American bison and to bully. All three

are used in this celebrated sentence, the longest grammatically correct sentence in English using just one word. Buffalo buffalo Buffalo buffalo buffalo buffalo Buffalo buffalo. It can be understood as 'Buffalo bison, that other Buffalo bison bully, also bully Buffalo bison.' An extreme example of ANTANACLASIS.

BULLDOZER a sleeping steer.

BUMBLEBEE a large bee which was originally called a humblebee because of the loud humming noise it made.

BUMF a disparaging term for paperwork, official papers or trashy literature. An abbreviation of BUMFODDER meaning toilet paper.

BUNGALOW comes from the Hindi *bangla* meaning a house in the style of Bengal. The story that it was made up by an Irish builder who said, 'bung a low roof on it.' is fictitious.

BURKE to Burke somebody is to murder them and sell their body to a medical school. Called after the Irishman William Burke who with his fellow criminal William Hare, dug up the bodies of executed criminals and sold them to the Anatomy Department of the Medical School of

Edinburgh University for dissection by students. But when the supply of such bodies dried up, they took to murdering people whose bodies they sold to the School. They were eventually caught, but Hare turned Queen's evidence to save his life and betrayed his friend. Burke was executed and ironically his body wound up in the medical school he had supplied.

BURPEE a squat thrust used as a full body strength training and as an aerobic exercise. Named in the 1930s for US physiologist Royal H. Burpee and popularized by the US Armed Services.

BUSTARD a bird which is neither one thing nor the other.

A Kori Bustard

BUTT this word has at least eight different meanings. To strike. A ridge between furrows. A flatfish. A mark for archery practice. A cask for wine. The thick end of an object. A cigarette end. A posterior.

BUTTERCUP a delightful flower which gets its name from the belief that if cows grazed where it grew, then their milk produced better butter. Some farmers believed that the colour of the buttercup gave the butter its colour.

BUZZARD an American term for a score on a golf hole which is two over par. Called a double bogey in Europe.

BYTE a unit of digital information in a computer, consisting of eight bits. A word coined in 1956 by computer scientist Werner Buchholz at IBM. A KILOBYTE is 1024 BYTES.

C

CALCULATE originally meant to compute with small pebbles, from which we get calculus. Also connected with calcareous – chalky or containing calcium carbonate. From the Latin *calculus* a little stone.

CALLIPYGEAN having large and shapely buttocks. From The ancient Greek, *kallos*, beauty and *puge*, buttocks. The word was used to discreetly describe a famous statue of Venus.

CAMELOPARD an old name for a giraffe. It was mistakenly believed it was a cross between a camel and a leopard, because of the shape of its head and its colouring.

CANARD a false rumour, a hoax. In French literally a duck.

CANARY ISLANDS they are named not after a bird but a dog. When Roman navigators discovered the islands, they found large dogs there. The Latin for dogs is *canaria*. When the English arrived many centuries later, they found some small birds which they named after the islands, CANARIES.

CANCAN an erotic dance associated with Paris. So-called because the movements of the girls' bottoms resemble those of ducks. See CANARD.

CAPACITIVE a modern word relating to a touchscreen that works by sensing when something that conducts electricity, such as a fingertip, is in contact with the screen.

CAPELLA a song sung without instrumental accompaniment – literally as in a chapel.

CAPERCAILLIE a large woodland grouse found in Scotland and other parts of Europe. In Gaelic *capull coille* means horse of the wood.

CAPPUCCINO this coffee is so-called because its colour supposedly resembles that of the brown hoods of the Capuchin Friars – an order of monks.

CAPTCHA you have probably see the little tests on webpages to see if you are a robot or not. The word is an acronym for Completely Automated Public Turing test to tell Computers and Humans Apart.

CARBUNCLE an inflammatory lump on the body, but also a beautiful precious stone. From the Latin *carbunculus*, a small coal.

CARCINIZATION is an example of convergent evolution in which a crustacean evolves into a crab-like form from a non-crab-like form. Crustaceans have evolved into the shape of a crab at least five independent times. From the Greek *karkinos* the crab.

CARPETBAGGER a political candidate, especially in the United States, who has no connection with the area in which he seeks election. The word comes from the fact that he carried his belongings in a carpetbag, and it has become synonymous with an unscrupulous opportunist.

CARRAGEEN a kind of seaweed used as a medicine for chest complaints. From the Irish *carraigin*, a little rock, on which the plant grows.

CARRINGTON EVENT a powerful geomagnetic storm in 1859, observed and recorded by British astronomers Richard Carrington and Richard Hodgson. It involved a huge solar coronal mass ejection. A solar storm of this magnitude occurring today would cause widespread electrical disruptions, blackouts and damage due to extended outages of the electrical grid.

CARTHORSE is an anagram of ORCHESTRA.

CASHMERE is a very fine soft wool. So called because it comes from goats raised in Kashmir in the Himalayas.

CASTANET to go fishing.

CASTOREUM a bitter, brown strong-smelling substance obtained from the perineum (an area close to the rectum) of beavers. Formerly used in medicine and perfumery. From the Greek *kastor*, beaver.

CAT the Chinese word for cat is miao.

CATCHFART a fawning servant who follows his master or mistress very closely and obsequiously.

CATCHPHRASE contains six consecutive consonants.

CATERWAUL to make a harsh cry. The dreadful noise made by cats at mating time. The word goes back to the time of Chaucer and may be a corruption of CAT and WAIL.

CATGUT dried intestines of sheep and cattle used for strings in musical instruments and old tennis racquets. The CAT probably comes from CATTLE so cat lovers can rest easy.

CATHEDRAL comes from the Latin for chair, *cathedra*. It is the church of the bishop and of the bishop's chair.

Florence Cathedral

CATTLE originally meant property from the Old French *chatel* from which we also get chattel. It came to mean livestock. CATTLE is a plural word which has no singular form. See SCISSORS.

CAT'S WHISKERS something which is exceptionally good. In the 1920s when crystal wireless sets were in vogue, the sensitive fine wires that made contact with the crystal were known as the cat's whiskers. The more sensitive they were, the better the reception.

CAULIFLOWER is the only vegetable which contains every vowel once and only once.

CAUWOT an acronym for Complete and Utter Waste of Time, such as Sudoku puzzles.

CEDILLA the little mark written under c in Spanish. Also used in French, Portuguese and other languages. From the Greek word for z which was the symbol originally used.

CELIBATE technically, this means unmarried, but it is often used in the sense of not engaging in sexual activity, which is not quite the same thing.

CHALK and CHEESE. A description of two things which are judged to have nothing in common. But chalk and cheese are both rich in calcium.

CHAMELEON a lizard capable of changing the colour of its skin to camouflage itself and whose eyes can move independently. There are over 200 separate species of chameleon. The word has come to be applied to people who change their appearance, opinions or outlook to suit the situation. From the Greek *khamaileon*, a compound of *khamai* on the ground and *leon* lion. So a ground lion.

CHAUVINIST a person who is excessively and irrationally patriotic. Nicholas Chauvin was a simple French soldier who had served under Napoleon, whom he worshipped despite all his faults. In more recent times, a 'male chauvinist pig' is a man who is totally biased against women.

CHECKMATE comes from the Persian *shah mat* meaning the king is dead.

CHEMISTRY is of Arabic origin. Its root is the word ALCHEMY from the Arabic *Al Kemia* meaning the Egyptian way. Many ancient methods came from Egypt.

CHIASMUS a figure of speech where the second part is the reverse of the first. E.g. Do not live to eat, but eat to live. From the Greek *chiasma*, a cross.

CHICAGO the name Chicago is derived from the local Indian word *chicagoua* meaning stinky garlic.

CHILIAHEDRON a polyhedron with a thousand plane surfaces - hard to distinguish from a sphere.

CHIPMUNK a French friar.

CHIROPRACTOR an Egyptian doctor.

CHOCOLATE comes from Nahuatl, the language of the Aztecs of central America.

CHORTLE to chuckle, to utter a gleeful laugh. Coined in 1871 by Lewis Carroll in 'Through the Looking Glass' and 'Jabberwocky'. Perhaps from chuckle and snort.

CHRISTIANITY is an anagram of I CRY THAT I SIN.

CHTHONIAN – pronounced thonian – is the only word which starts with four consecutive consonants. It means pertaining to the underworld.

CHUNDER Australian slang for to throw up. When doing this on a ship, it was only polite to warn people down below who might have their heads sticking out of a porthole. 'Watch under' was the cry, which was shortened to chunder.

CHUNNEL a PORTMANTEAU word for the undersea tunnel under the Channel between England and France.

CHUTZPAH nerve, audacity or effrontery. From the Yiddish *khutspe*, impudence. The classic definition is that given by Leo Rosten: 'that quality of a man who, having killed his mother and father, throws himself on the mercy of the court because he is an orphan.'

CIAO mediaeval Italians would politely greet one another with the expression *'Sono vostro schiavo'* meaning 'I am your servant' or even 'I am your slave'. This was shortened to *Schiavo* and then to *Ciao*.

CICATRICE a scar resulting from a wound. From the Latin *cicatrix*, a scar.

CIPHER originally a word for zero but it came to mean any numeral. Also, secret writing or a code. From the Arabic *sifr*, zero.

CIRCUMLOCUTION too many words. Expressing an idea in more words than are necessary. 'Roundabout' speech. From the Latin *circum*, around *locutus*, spoken. Dickens invented the Circumlocution Office in Little Dorrit.

CLAUSTROPHOBIA fear of Father Christmas.

CLAQUE a group of people hired to applaud in a theatre. From the French *claquer* to clap. Not to be confused with CLIQUE, a small exclusive party, a coterie.

CLODHOPPER a humorously abusive name for a rustic or country dweller who could not afford a horse or carriage and who had to avoid the water and mud by hopping from clod to clod.

CLEAVE has two separate and opposite meanings - to join or to split. From the German *kleben* to stick. It is a CONTRANYM.

CLIMATE what you do to a ladder.

CLUE comes from the Middle English word *clewe* meaning a ball of yarn or thread.

COACH a word of Hungarian origin. From *kocsi*, a horse-drawn wagon with springs above the axles. Named after the Hungarian village of Kocs where this type of vehicle was invented. The verb to coach also comes from this root.

COCKNEY a native of the city of London, specifically someone born within the sound of Bow bells. The name comes from Middle English words meaning 'cock's egg', a name given to a small or distorted egg, the runt of the clutch, laid not by the hen but by the cock.

COLPORTEUR a street seller of religious books and trinkets. From the Latin *comportare*, to carry. Possibly the inspiration for the name of the great composer, Cole Porter.

CONCOCT to make up a story or an excuse. From the Latin *concoquere*, to cook together.

COOKIE is from the Dutch *koekje*, which is a diminutive form of their word for cake, *koek*.

CLOVEN means divided into two, as in a cloven hoof. It is the past participle of CLEAVE.

COFFEE from Ottoman Turkish *kahve*, coffee, from Arabic *qahwa*, a brew. The Arabic word originally referred to wine, a drink traditionally served hot in a similar manner to coffee.

COFFIN NAIL a slang word for a cigarette, in use long before the deadly effects of smoking were discovered by medical experimenters.

COLLYWOBBLES abdominal pain, nervous stomach or a general state of apprehensiveness. Probably from colic and wobble.

COMA has a spurious acronym - Cessation Of Motor Activity.

COMEUPPANCE a deserved rebuke or penalty, when someone gets their just desserts.

COMMANDO a word introduced into the language by Winston Churchill. He may have heard it as a young soldier in South Africa where it is the Afrikaans word for a troop under a commander. The expression going commando means not wearing underwear and so ready for action.

COMMITTEE contains three pairs of double letters.

COMPANION was originally someone you shared bread with. From the Latin *cum* with and *panis* bread.

CONCENTRALIZATION the action or fact of becoming concentrated at a common centre. An impressive word to use at your next business meeting.

CONFABULATE to talk familiarly together, to chat. But in psychiatry, it means to fill in gaps in memory by fabrication. From the Latin *fabula*, story, which is also the root of fable and fabulous.

CONSTELLATE to gather together in a cluster or group. From the Latin *con*, together and *stellatus*, like a star.

CONTRANYM a word that has two opposite meanings.
See CLEAVE and SANCTION.

CONVERSATIONALISTS is an anagram of
CONSERVATIONALISTS and at 18 letters these are the
two longest single word anagrams (excluding obscure
medical terms). That is something to bring up in your
next conversation.

COPROLITE a fossil consisting of petrified excrement,
particularly of a dinosaur; a lovely house ornament and
conversation piece. From the Greek *kopros*, dung.

CORDUROY a thick cotton material with raised parallel
lines. From the French, *Cord du Roi*, meaning cloth of the
king. Corduroy pillows make headlines.

CORMORANT a shiny black fish-eating bird originally
known as a sea raven. The name comes from the
Latin *corvus marinus* sea crow.

CORONER a stiff examiner.

CORPULENT stout or fat. From the Latin *corpus*, body
and *ulentus*, full of. In 1812 Leigh Hunt was sent to

prison for two years for calling the Prince Regent corpulent in print.

COSSET a pet lamb reared by hand. From which we get cosseted, meaning spoiled or overindulged.

COSTERMONGER a fruit seller. A costard is a large variety of apple and *mango* is Latin for a dealer. Other such words are fishmonger, ironmonger, scandalmonger, whoremonger and cheesemonger.

COUP DE GRACE French term for a lawn mower.

COUSCOUS is the longest word which looks the same in capitals and lower-case letters. A word of Moroccan and Arabic origin.

COVID 19 is a sort of acronym for Coronavirus Disease 2019. The word was coined in 2020.

COWARD a coward was originally a boy who looked after cows.

CRABCAKE and DABCHICK are, we think, the only words containing the block abc.

CRACKBERRY a term for a person addicted to using their Blackberry.

CRAIC a good time, fun, a convivial atmosphere. From Hiberno-English, a dialect used in Ireland.

CRAPULENCE is sickness caused by excessive drinking. When you are hung-over you feel crapulent.

CRAWL is the name for the rolling credits at the end of a film or TV show.

CREPUSCULAR a very beautiful word referring to twilight (*crespusculum* in Latin is twilight).

CROCODILE supposedly named from its habit of basking in the sun on the shores of the river Nile. The name means literally 'pebble worm' in Latin.

CROQUETTE a tiny crocodile.

CROW the collective name for a group of crows is a 'murder'.

CRUCIVERBALIST a crossword addict. From the Latin *crux* cross and *verbum* word.

CRYTOSCOPOPHILIA an irresistible urge to look in the windows of houses you are passing.

CUL-DE-SAC a dead-end street; French for bottom of a bag.

CUNEIFORM wedge-shaped. Usually applied to the characters of ancient Persian inscriptions.

CURFEW was a signal to extinguish fires and lights. From Old French *cuevrefeu*, cover fire.

CURMUDGEON an ill-tempered person, a churlish fellow, a miser.

CUSHION is one of only two common words ending in -SHION. The other is FASHION.

CUSHY easy, not entailing difficulty. Anglo Indian slang from the Hindi word *khush*, pleasant.

CUSPIDOR a beautiful word, but how do you feel when you are told it is another word for a spittoon?

CYBERSQUATTING the registering particular terms as Internet domain names, in the hope of reselling them at a profit.

CYPRUS takes its name from its many copper mines which have been mined for thousands of years. The Greek word for copper is *kypros*.

CYRILLIC an alphabet used in Russia and parts of Eastern Europe. It is named after Saint Cyril, a 9th-century missionary who devised the system to translate the Bible into the languages of the Slavic peoples.

D

DACHSHUND originally a dog for hunting badgers, because its long low body was ideal for entering badger setts. From German words meaning 'badger hound'. Sometimes called a sausage dog because of its shape.

DACTYLONOMY is the art of counting on one's fingers. DACTYLOLOGY is the art of talking with one's fingers. i.e. sign language. From the Greek *daktylos* a finger.

DAGUERREOTYPE one of the earliest practical photographic processes invented by Louis Daguerre (1789-1851). In the daguerreotype, an image was produced on iodine-sensitized silver and developed in a mercury vapour.

DALTONISM congenital colour-blindness, especially with regard to red, green, orange and brown. It is called after John Dalton (1766-1844) an English chemist who formulated the atomic theory and suffered from this condition.

DANDELION is from the French *dent de lion* meaning lion's tooth.

DASTARD a mean and contemptuous coward who commits foul acts without endangering himself.

DASYPYGAL having hairy buttocks. Used to describe types of ape (but feel free to apply it to people you know). From Greek *dasus*, hairy and *puge*, buttocks.

DATASTROPHE when your computer crashes and everything gets wiped out.

DAUPHIN the term for the eldest son of the King of France, means dolphin because his coat of arms had three dolphins.

DEBACLE a failure, collapse or fiasco. The first five letters of debacle are the first five letters of the alphabet a b c d e. The word originally meant the breaking of ice or the rush of water which followed.

DEBATE what attracts de fish.

DECAY how can you spell deterioration with just two letters? DK.

DECIBEL the measurement of the loudness of sound. It was named after Alexander Graham Bell, the inventor of the telephone.

DECIMATE to do great harm or damage to. From the Roman practice of killing one person in ten as a punishment or reprisal.

DECOLLETAGE the low-cut neckline of a dress comes from a French word meaning 'exposing the neck' (and maybe other things as well!).

DEFCON is short for Defence Condition. One of five levels of U.S. military defence readiness that are ranked according to the perceived threat to national security.

DEFENESTRATION is the act of throwing someone out of the window. From the Latin *de,* from and *fenestra,* window.

DEMI means half and so do HEMI and SEMI.

DENIAL a river in Egypt.

DENIM this strong cotton material takes its name from Nimes in France. It was originally known as DeNimes.

DERMATOLOGIST a doctor who makes rash decisions.

DEODOND in mediaeval times, something which caused the death of a person and was therefore forfeited to the church for holy purposes. From Latin *deo,* to God and *dandum,* to be given.

DERRICK a long beam used for lifting heavy objects. Named after the hangman Thomas Derrick who lived around 1600.

DESSERTS is the longest word which forms another word when spelled backwards, STRESSED.

DETARTRATED something from which tartrates (salts of tartaric acid) have been removed. Like AIBOHPHOBIA it is an eleven letter PALINDROME. They are the longest single word palindromes we know of.

DIARRHOEA is a very difficult word to spell, but here is a MNEMONIC to help you remember: Dash in a rush, run hard or else accident.

DIASTEMA is a gap between the front teeth. Many species of mammals have a diastema as a normal feature, most commonly between the incisors and molars.

The actor Terry Thomas displaying his diastema

DICE is the plural of DIE, a cube with pips on its six faces used in games and gambling. DIES is also a legitimate plural.

DIGERATI people who are experts with information technology. A combination of digital and literati.

DICKENS an old word for the devil. The phrase 'What the Dickens' was used by Shakespeare long before the birth of the great novelist Charles Dickens.

DIGIT a finger, from the Latin *digitus*, finger or toe. Also, a number such as 1, 6, or 8. Perhaps the Romans liked counting on their fingers.

DINKY an acronym standing for Double Income No Kids Yet. A useful marketing categorization. On the other hand, DINKUM stands for Double Income No Kids, Unbelievable Mortgage.

DIPLOMAT from diploma which comes from a Greek word meaning a piece of paper folded double.

DIRGE a slow mournful song of lamentation. From the opening Latin words of the first psalm, *Dirige Domine*, 'Direct, O Lord.'

DISCIPLINE meaning punishment, training or a system of rules comes from the same root as disciple – the Latin word *discipulus*, pupil or follower.

DISCOMBOBULATE to upset or disconcert. Origin unknown.

DISINGENUOUS a frequently used but often misunderstood word. It means untruthful, crafty or devious. Ingenuous means frank, free or artless. An ingenue is a naïve and innocent young woman. From the Latin *ingenuus* free born.

DISMAL gloomy or dreary but originally dismal meant an unlucky day. From the Latin *dies mali,* evil days. In the Middle Ages, calendars marked as unlucky two days of each month (Jan. 1, 25; Feb. 4, 26; March 1, 28; April 10, 20; May 3, 25; June 10, 16; July 13, 22; Aug. 1, 30; Sept. 3, 21; Oct. 3, 22; Nov. 5, 28; Dec. 7, 22), supposedly based on the ancient calculations of Egyptian astrologers

DJIBOUTI (pronounced ja booty) is a country in the east of Africa. It has the smallest population (under 1m) and the strangest name of any African country. There are very few words beginning dj but others include DJINN, a spirit or genii, and DJELLABA, a hooded cloak. All these words are of Arabic origin.

DOCTOR literally a teacher from the Latin *docere* to teach. Stolen from academia by the medics.

DOG the word for dog in the extinct and ancient Aboriginal language of Mbaram is DOG.

DOGMA a hound's mother.

DOLDRUMS to be in the doldrums is to be depressed or downhearted. From a region near the Equator in the Atlantic Ocean which experiences long periods of calm causing sailing ships to stall.

DONTOPEDALOGY is the venerable art of putting your foot in your mouth. The word was coined by the Duke of Edinburgh, who was guilty of it on occasions.

DOPPLEGANGER an apparition, often ominous, which is a double of a living person. From the German word *doppelgänger,* meaning double goer.

DORMOUSE a rodent which is not strictly speaking a mouse but is like a mouse. It hibernates for a long time and has a reputation for being sleepy. So the French called it a *dormeuse* – meaning she who sleeps. In English that became dormouse.

DORMY or DORMIE a situation in match play golf where one player leads by the number of holes left to play and therefore cannot lose (but could draw). According to the USGA Museum, the term is a corruption of the French word *dormir*, to sleep. Perhaps the player who is dormie can now relax or go to sleep.

DOUCEUR a financial inducement or bribe. Literally a sweetness in French.

DOWN you cannot get DOWN from a camel; but you can from a duck.

DOZENS has seven letters but if you remove one letter you are left with twelve.

DRACONIAN a very severe law is often described as draconian, after a Greek law maker named Draco who lived around 620 B C. For example, he decreed that people found urinating in public should be executed.

DRACULA comes from the Irish *Droc Fhola*, meaning bad blood.

DRAGOON originally a musket which 'breathed fire like a dragon.' It came to mean a cavalry soldier.

DREAMT is the only word ending in MT.

DREICH a Scottish word meaning miserable, cold, damp weather. Anything tedious or dreary.

DRUNK is the word with the most synonyms in the English language. There are more than three thousand of them, including stocious, blotto, hammered, tipsy, rat-arsed and see TROLLIED.

DUCK in cricket a duck is a score of 0. It was originally a duck's egg, which looks like a 0. This was shortened to duck.

DUDGEON a feeling of offence, resentment or sullen anger. Often used in the phrase 'in high dudgeon'. Low dudgeon seems to be unknown.

DUFFLE COATS are named after the town of Duffel in Belgium where the coats were originally made.

DUMBBELL one of a pair of weighted bars used for exercise. When training for campanology or bell ringing, beginners made such an unholy racket, that they were obliged to use bells without tongues which made no noise. They were called dumb bells.

DUNCE an obsolete and nowadays politically incorrect word for a slow-learning child. The dunce's cap was placed on the child's head and he was banished into a corner. John Duns Scotus (1265-1308) was a great scholastic philosopher whose opponents and enemies used his name as a term of abuse.

DWAAL a dreamy, dazed, or absent-minded state. From Afrikaans.

DZO a Tibetan word for a male hybrid between the yak and domestic cattle. The female is known as a dzomo or zhom.

EARWIG so called from the ancient false belief that the garden pest went into people's ears and ate their brains!

EBONY is a dense black hardwood. It sinks in water. The word ebony comes from the Ancient Egyptian *hbny*.

ECLIPSE what a London barber does.

ECTOPLASM a biological term for the outer layer of a cell. It also denotes a noxious substance supposedly emanating from the body of a medium during a spiritual trance. Others claim it is the stuff that ghosts are made of.

ECUADOR is so named because its capital, Quito, lies on the equator. The word equator comes from the Latin *equalis* (equal) because it is an imaginary line which divides the Earth into two equal halves.

EDAM is the only cheese which is made backwards.

EDAMAME is Japanese for beans on a branch.

EEJIT idiot. From Hiberno-English.

EERIE and EEL two of the very few words in English that begin with EE.

EFFEMINATELY is the longest word one can make with capital letters composed of straight lines.

EGGCORN a word or phrase that sounds like and is mistakenly used in a seemingly logical or plausible way for another word or phrase. E.g. saying 'for all intensive purposes' when you mean 'for all intents and purposes.' Coined in 2003 by Professor Geoffrey Pullum after a woman used egg corn instead of acorn.

EGGS as sure as eggs is eggs is a corruption of as sure as x = x, i.e., mathematically and logically certain.

EGREGIOUS outstanding, conspicuously bad or flagrant. From the Latin *ex grege,* out of the flock.

EGYPTOLOGIST a mummy's boy who digs older women.

EIFFEL TOWER in Paris is named after its architect, Gustave Eiffel (1832-1923). He also designed the interior structure of the Statue of Liberty in New York.

EIGENGRAU is the name of the shade of dark grey that you see when you open your eyes in a pitch-black room.

EINSTEIN pointed out that his name twice broke the rule; I before E except after C. DEFICIENCIES is another double culprit.

EINSTEINIUM element number 99 is named after Albert Einstein. Other element eponyms include Curium (96), Mendelevium (101) and Rutherfordium (104).

ELLIPTICAL a kiss.

EMBARRASSING, MILLENNIUM and SEPARATE are three of the most frequently misspelled words in the English language.

EMERALD a green gemstone. Most emeralds are mined in Colombia. Carat for carat it is the most valuable precious stone.

EMORDNILAP a word which when spelled backwards gives another word. Examples are flog and golf or drawer and reward. No prizes for seeing that emordnilap is the reverse of PALINDROME.

EMOTICON a group of keyboard characters (such as :-)) that typically represents a facial expression. An emotional icon. EMOTICONS is an anagram of ECONOMIST.

ENAMEL the hardest substance in the human body is tooth enamel.

ENCYCLOPEDIA from the Greek *enkyklios paideia* meaning the cycle of training of children.

ENDLING the final individual in a species which becomes extinct.

ENDORSE last in the race.

ENGINEER as in Civil Engineer or Electrical Engineer, is not connected with the word engine at all. It is derived fom *ingenieur*, a French word for an ingenious or clever person. However, in the USA, the person who drives the engine of a train is called an engineer.

ENGLAND means land of the Angles. The Angles were one of the main Germanic tribes who settled in Great Britain in the post-Roman period.

ENUMERATION is an anagram of MOUNTAINEER.

EPENTHESIS the insertion of an extra sound (or word) into a word. E.g. saying 'athalete' instead of athlete or 'fillum' for film. Or inserting your chosen expletive into abso ******* lutely.

EPHEMERAL a beautiful word meaning short-lived or fleeting, literally lasting only one day, like a mayfly. From the Greek *epi*, for and *hemera*, a day.

EPONYM someone whose name is given to a title, thing or action. Or the thing itself. From Greek *eponymos* giving one's name to something. How many eponyms can you find in this book?

EQUINOX the time when the sun crosses the equator making the night equal in length to the day. Usually,

March 21 and September 23. From the Latin *aequus,* equal and *nox,* night.

EREWHON is the title of a book about an idealised country by Samuel Butler. The title is an anagram of NOWHERE.

ESTIVAL (or AESTIVAL) means of summer. Estivation is the opposite of hibernation and describes the state of some insects (and teenagers) who spend the summer in a state of torpor. From the Latin *aestivus* summer.

ESPERANTO an artificial international language devised by the Polish linguist, Dr Ludwig Zamenhof in 1887. Esperanto means 'hopeful' in Esperanto.

ETYMON the true origin of a word, the original root. Etymology the study of the derivation of words comes from the same Greek word, *etymos,* true.

EUNUCH a man cut out to be a bachelor.

EUREKA is what they said to Archimedes before he took a bath. Eureka is the motto of the State of California. In

Greek it means 'I have found it' and refers to the discovery of gold there.

EVEREST the world's highest mountain is named after Sir George Everest (1709-1866) the first Surveyor General of India. But Sir George never saw the mountain; it was named in his honour by his colleagues after his death.

Mount Everest

EVITATIVE referring to something to be feared or avoided. Another nice PALINDROME.

EWE and YOU have the same pronunciation but have no letters in common.

EXAGGERATE to overstate one thousand-fold.

EXITS are certainly on the way out.

EXPECTORATE if you expectorate, you cannot expect to rate. Another example of ANTANACLASSIS.

EXPERT someone with a special skill, knowledge or mastery. From the Latin *expertus*, tested or shown to be true. However, cynics point out that ex is a has been and a spurt is a drip under pressure.

FAHRENHEIT the first effective temperature scale, invented by Gabriel Fahrenheit (1686-1736). It set 32 degrees F for the melting point of ice and 212 degrees F for the boiling point of water. It is still used in the United States, but most of the rest of the world have replaced it with the Celsius scale. It is believed that Fahrenheit chose his scale so that the normal human temperature would be 100F, but he miscalibrated. It came out at 98.4 degrees F.

FAST has two contradictory meanings. A fast horse runs, but a fast colour does not. A CONTRANYM.

FAUCET what you have to do when a door is stuck. Or maybe you should just give it a tap!

FAULCONBRIDGE an Australian town whose name uses half of the alphabet, including all five vowels and does not repeat a single letter.

FEEDBACK is the shortest word containing the first six letters of the alphabet.

FEISTY means spirited and exuberant, but it comes from the Middle English word *fisten* meaning to fart.

FERRET the name of this nasty animal comes from the Latin *furritus*, meaning a little thief, because of its habit of stealing birds' eggs.

FIACRE a small four-wheeled horse drawn carriage used in Paris around 1700. It was called after Saint Fiacre, an Irish monk who founded a monastery in France in 670. Saint Fiacre is the patron saint of haemorrhoids; whether to acquire them or get rid of them is not clear.

FIJI the original International Dateline went right through the middle of Fiji, so the inhabitants had it bent so that they could all share the same day.

FILIBUSTER originally a filibuster was a pirate or buccaneer. It was adopted in US politics to describe someone who hijacks proceedings and obstructs legislation by making extremely lengthy speeches. Derived from freebooter which came from the German *frei* free and *buit* booty.

FINLAND a shark-based theme park.

FISHMONGER someone who knows his plaice.

FIVE-FINGER DISCOUNT a euphemism for shoplifting.

FLAMMABLE and INFLAMMABLE both mean the same thing - capable of burning.

FLAK comes from the German where it was an acronym for *Flug Abwehr Kanone* meaning anti-aircraft gun.

FLIBBERTIGIBBET a flighty gossip. A silly person who talks too much.

FLEAS the subject of the shortest poem ever written; Adam, 'Ad 'em.

FLOTSAM and JETSAM are often confused. Flotsam is wreckage found floating in the water whereas jetsam is goods thrown overboard from a ship to lighten it and often found washed ashore. From the old French *floter* to float and a contraction of jettison from the Latin *jacere* to throw.

FLOTUS stands for First Lady of the United States, the wife of the POTUS.

FLOWER NAMES there are at least twenty names of flowers and plants which are also women's first names. These include Ivy, Pansy, Rose, Violet, Hyacinth, Lily and Heather. No men's names immediately spring to mind.

FLOWER and FLOUR these were originally the same word. Flour was the best part of the grain, the flower.

FLUEOLOGIST a fancy name for a chimney sweep.

FLYER and BOOMER a female kangaroo is called a Flyer and a male kangaroo is called a Boomer. What a charming couple!

FOMO an acronym for Fear of Missing Out.

FOND in the 14th century this word meant insane or deranged. It came to mean foolish, then foolishly tender and thence to the current meaning of having an affection for.

FONTANELLE babies are born with a soft spot on the top of the skull to allow for growth and expansion. The fontanelle usually has closed by the time the baby is a year and a half. From Old French, meaning 'a little fountain'.

FOOLSCAP a formerly common paper size bigger than A4. It is so called because its watermark contained a jester's cap.

FORMICA a plastic laminated product which was originally an artificial substitute FOR MICA, a shiny mineral used in table tops and counters.

FORMICARY an anthill, from the Latin *formica*, an ant. FORMICATION is the creepy feeling that insects are crawling on your skin.

FOUR is the only number whose value is the same as the number of letters it contains.

FREE WILL we have got to believe in free will; we have no choice.

FREELANCE originally a mediaeval mercenary, a knight whose lance was free to hire.

FREQUENCY Q is the least used letter in English, and E is the most used letter. The most frequent initial letter is S, and the least frequent is X.

FRISBEE a plastic disk that you throw as a game. The name comes from Mrs. Frisbie's Pies, made by the Frisbie Bakery of Bridgeport, Connecticut, whose pie tins her young employees started to throw about in the 1930s.

FROMOLOGY the hobby of collecting cheese labels. From *fromage*, French for cheese.

FULL is the only word ending in 'full'. All others such as 'blissful' end in a single l.

FUNAMBULIST a tightrope walker. From the Latin *funis* rope and *ambulare* to walk.

FUNERAL is an anagram of REAL FUN.

FURLONG one eighth of a mile, now used only in horse racing. It comes from furrow-long, the length that a good horse was expected to plough in a day.

FUTTOCK one of the curved timbers used to make the rib on the hull of a wooden ship.

G

GAIT the distinctive bearing or method of walking of a person or animal. Probably from the Old Norse *gata* way or path.

GALAXY a spiralling system of stars. The word comes from the Greek word for milk, *galaxias kyklos*, literally milky circle. The Milky Way was the first galaxy to be named by astronomers.

GALLIVANT to roam around for pleasure, to gad about.

GALLON a ten-gallon hat can hold about 6 pints of water – so less than a gallon.

GALLIUM a metal which melts at around 40 degrees centigrade and it will liquefy in your hand. It was discovered in 1875 but its existence was predicted in 1871 by Russian chemist Dmitri Mendeleev, who named it "eka-aluminium" from its position in his theory of the periodic table. Its discovery helped confirm the validity of Mendeleev's great idea.

GAMP a name for an umbrella. Called after Mrs. Sarah Gamp, a character in the novel Martin Chuzzlewit by Charles Dickens, who was rarely seen without one.

GARDEN has three anagrams – DANGER, GANDER, and RANGED.

GARDYLOO a shout formerly used by Scottish housewives. It was a warning that liquid was about to be thrown from the premises into the street. It is derived from the French gardez *l'eau*, beware of the water.

GAUNTLET to run the gauntlet was a form of military corporal punishment in which a man was forced to run between two rows of soldiers, who struck and beat him. In this case the word gauntlet has nothing to do with the armoured glove but was an EGGCORN for the Swedish *gatlopp*, from *gata* lane and *lopp* running.

GAZUMP to raise the price of a property after previously accepting an offer. From the Yiddish *gezumph* – to swindle.

GAZUNDER a chamber pot, because it goes under the bed. It can also mean to lower the price of your offer just before contracts are due to be signed (see GAZUMP).

GESTALT an entity which is perceived be more than the sum of its parts. From the German *Gestalt*, a form or shape.

GEYSIR an individual geyser in Iceland which was the first geyser described in a printed source and gives its name to all other geysers worldwide. It is spectacular, shooting boiling water up to 200 feet in the air.

Iceland Geysir

GIBBOUS hump-shaped, swollen. Often used to describe the moon when between a half moon and a full moon.

GIGO a computer acronym for Garbage In, Garbage Out. But it is possible to start with a false statement, apply the laws of logic correctly, and deduce a true statement. E.g. assume that 2 = 3, which is certainly false. Now if 2 = 3, then 3 = 2, and adding these equations together, we get 2 + 3 = 3 + 2, or 5=5, which is a correct statement. But you will be relieved to hear that starting off with a true statement, and using the laws of logic, it is not possible to deduce a false statement.

GINGLYFORM an obscure word meaning shaped like a hinge.

GINORMOUS very big indeed. A PORTMANTEAU word formed from gigantic and enormous.

GLASS SLIPPERS Cinderella did not wear glass slippers. The misunderstanding arose from a mistranslation of the French for fur which is *vair*, as *verre*, which is glass.

GLITCH a malfunction, often in a machine or in a block of code. Derived from the Yiddish *glitsh,* meaning a slip.

GOAT the best butter.

GOBBLEDEGOOK unintelligible jargon, nonsense. The word was invented in 1944 by US politician, Maury Maverick, and first used to describe a text riddled with jargon and complicated sentence structures. A SYNONYM is BAFFLEGAB.

GOBEMOUCHE someone who believes everything they are told. It comes from the French for flycatcher.

GOBSHITE someone who talks rubbish, a stupid person, an EEJIT. From Hiberno-English.

GOOGLE the company founded by Larry Page and Sergey Brin. The name originated from a misspelling of the word GOOGOL, which was picked to signify that the search engine was intended to provide large quantities of information.

GOOGOL an incredibly large number; 10 to the power 100, written as 1 followed by 100 zeroes. The term was coined in 1920 by 9-year-old Milton Sirotta, nephew of U.S. mathematician Edward Kasner. The total number of sub-atomic particles in the Universe is thought to be less than a GOOGOL.

GOOGOLPLEX the number 10 to the power of a GOOGOL. It is an unimaginably large number. Carl Sagan gave an example that if the entire volume of the observable universe is filled with fine dust particles roughly 1.5 micrometres in size (0.0015 millimetres), then the number of different combinations in which the particles could be arranged would be about one googolplex.

GORMLESS, FECKLESS, RUTHLESS AND RECKLESS are all negative versions of words that were once used but are now lost. Gorm meant sense, feck effect, ruth regret, and reck awareness.

GOTCHA an attempt to embarrass, expose, or disgrace someone (such as a politician). A colloquial contraction of 'I have got you'.

GRAFFITI, PAPPARAZZI, TIMPANI and SCAMPI are all Italian plurals. The singulars are almost never used in English – graffito, paparazzo, timpano and scampo.

GREENLAND is covered in ice and snow but was named Greenland by the Norse explorer Erik the Red supposedly to make it sound attractive to settlers. It is an early example of misleading advertising. Greenland is the largest island in the world with an area of 2.17 m square kilometres but a population of just 56,000. AUSTRALIA is larger but is classified as a continental land mass.

GREMLIN an imaginary mischievous spirit believed to inhabit machinery and cause it to malfunction especially when it is most needed. First coined by the Royal Air Force in relation to their airplanes.

GROCER this word was originally spelled GROSSER, referring to a person who bought in gross and sold retail.

GUBBINS a trivial object, a gadget or device. Also, a silly or foolish person.

GUILLOTINE named after its EPONYM, Dr Joseph-Ignace Guillotin, who in France in 1789 proposed that this device be used for capital punishment. He believed that it was more efficient and humane than the methods previously used. During the Reign of Terror in 1793 and 1794 about 17,000 people were guillotined. It was last used in France in 1977.

GULLGROPER a greedy moneylender.

GULLIBLE when turned upside down this word looks like a reclining leopard. Simply rotate the book to observe this phenomenon.

GUNDYGUT a greedy person who eats too much. Other disparaging terms include a fatso, a porker, a salad-dodger, a pavement-cracker and a lard-arse.

GUM comes to us from the ancient Egyptians. They chewed resin from tree sap and called it *qmy* or *qemi*. They used the sap as a flavouring agent in food. The tomb of the grandparents of King Tut contained foods coated with gum.

GYMNASIUM an exercise club, a school. The word literally means to exercise in the nude. From Greek *gymnazein,* to exercise naked, from *gymnos,* naked.

H

HA-HA not as funny as you might think. A HA-HA is a name for a sunken fence or boundary which allows an uninterrupted view.

HAKA a traditional Maori dance often performed by New Zealand sports teams to intimidate opponents.

HALCYON felt by some to be the most beautiful word in the English language, both in terms of sound and meaning. Halcyon days denote remembered days of the past when all seemed happy and peaceful. In legend, Halcyon was a princess transformed into a kingfisher who calmed the wind and high seas into submission.

HALLOWEEN the evening before All Hallows or All Saints day in the Church calendar. HALLOW is to make holy.

HAM ACTOR   an untalented and impecunious theatrical performer who was forced to use ham fat to remove the makeup from his face.

HANDICAP a convenient hat.

HANKY-PANKY one of the many rhyming couplets beginning with the letter H. Examples include helter-skelter, harum-scarum, hocus-pocus, hotch-potch, hoity-toity and higgledy-piggledy. The correct term for these couplets is reduplicative but we think they should be called HURDY-WORDIES.

HAPAX LEGOMENON a word of which only one use is recorded in a work or body of work. E.g. Satyr, although a common word in English generally, is a hapax legomenon for Shakespeare as it occurs only once in his writings. From a Greek term meaning 'once said'.

HAPPY AS A SANDBOY sandboys were employed in Wild West bars to clean the floors by spreading sand on them and sweeping up. Sometimes they found coins that drunken cowboys had dropped and that made them very happy.

HATCHET what a bird tries to do when it sits on an egg. Chop chop.

HAUTBOY a wooden wind instrument with a high-pitched note; an old name for an oboe. From the French *haut*, high, and *bois*, wood.

HAVELOCK a cloth screen at the back of a soldier's cap to prevent sunburn on the neck. Named after Sir Henry Havelock, (1795-1857) a British General who fought in Afghanistan and India.

HEADMISTRESSSHIP is the only word with a triple S.

HEATHEN from a Norse word. The Vikings called those people who lived on the heath or open country *heidinn*.

HECKLE a heckle was a comb for taking knots out of flax. Hecklers were workers who did this. The hecklers of Dundee in Scotland were famous for their boisterous union meetings at which visitors were interrupted and badgered. Hence the modern meaning of HECKLE.

HELIOTROPE a wild plant flowering in winter. From Greek words meaning bending towards the sun.

HEROES what a man in a boat does.

HEROIN was created as a trademark by the German company Bayer for a new drug they created in 1898. The name was used because trials showed that the drug made people feel heroic. The product was supposed to be less addictive than morphine, but this proved not to be the case.

HERSTORY an alternative to history used by some feminists.

HEXADACTYLISM the condition of having six fingers or six toes on a hand or foot. From the Greek *hexa,* six and *daktylos,* finger.

HIBERNACLE a winter retreat, a shelter for an animal to hibernate. From the Latin *hibernacula*, winter quarters.

HIBERNIA the old Roman name for Ireland meaning land of winter.

HIJINKS the only word with three consecutive dotted letters - unless you include the country of Fiji.

HIMBO a handsome but stupid man. The male equivalent of BIMBO.

HIPPOCAMPUS a ridge on the ventricle of the brain, thought to be the centre of emotion and memory. Also, a sea-horse from the Greek *hippos,* a horse and *kampos,* a sea-monster.

HIPPOPOTAMUS this large African animal is literally a river horse; from the Greek, *hippos,* a horse and *potamos,* a river.

HOG an ancient word for a pig. HOGWASH was kitchen or brewery refuse given as food to pigs. It now means insincere rubbish. A hog with no legs is called a groundhog.

HOI POLLOI the vulgar, the masses, the rabble. In Greek *hoi polloi* means the many so to say 'the hoi polloi' is a TAUTOLOGY.

HOLLAND is a province on the western coast of the Netherlands. The name Holland is often used incorrectly to refer to the whole of the country even by the Dutch themselves.

HOMAGE an expression of high regard or respect. The root is Latin *homo,* man. In medieval times, a man could officially become the king's man or vassal by publicly announcing allegiance to the monarch. The ritual was known as homage.

HOMONYMNS words which are pronounced the same but have different spellings. Words with four homonyms include scents, cents, sense and cense and also right, write, rite and wright.

HONEYMOON the Babylonians decreed that mead, an alcoholic drink made from honey, was the official wedding drink. The bride's parents had an obligation to supply the groom with mead for up to a month after the wedding to keep up his strength. This was the honeymoon, a month of honey drink.

HORSESHOER and INTESTINES are unusual words in that each contains five different letters in its first five letters and the same five letters in a different order in its second five letters.

HOUSEWARMING is a lovely custom that began in Scotland. Embers from the last fire in a previous residence were carried to form the first fire in a new house.

HOUYHNHNM a horse endowed with reason, featured by Swift in Gulliver's Travels. The word was meant to imitate the neighing of a horse. The word has six consecutive consonants.

HUFFLEBUFFS a Scottish word for old, comfortable clothes worn about the house.

HULLABALOO an uproar, a commotion, a noisy racket. Derivation possibly from hallelujah or from hello hello.

A HUNT AND PECK is a guy who uses just one or two fingers on the keyboard.

HURRICANE comes from the Maya who believed in a 'god of the storm' called *Hunraken*. The word was used throughout Central America and the Caribbean to mean an evil deity. Spanish explorers used *huracan* to describe a storm.

HUSBAND comes from the Old Norse and means house dweller; *hus* house and *bondi* dweller.

HYACINTH what you say when you meet Cynthia.

HYDROPHOBIA a morbid fear of water; one of the symptoms of rabies. It was the first phobia to be given a name, way back in the 16th century.

HYSTERIA was originally defined as a neurotic condition peculiar to women and thought to be caused by a dysfunction of the uterus; from the Greek *hysterikos,* of the womb. So, by that logic, a man could not be HYSTERICAL just as a woman could show VIRTUE as that was the quality of a man, from the Latin *vir,* man.

HYPHENATED is non-hyphenated whereas non-hyphenated is hyphenated. A PARADOX.

I

I is the commonest word in spoken language.

IATROGENIC relating to an illness caused by surgeons or doctors. From the Greek *iatros*, a doctor.

ICONOCLAST someone who destroys images. Hence a rebellious person intent on tearing down structures. From the Greek *eikon*, image and *klastes*, breaker.

IGNORAMUS nowadays, a stupid person, but originally a jury verdict meaning 'we do not know' from the Latin *ignoramus*.

ILLEGAL a sick bird.

IOUEA a genus of sea sponges. The only word to contain all five vowels and no other letter.

IMPECCABLE one of the many words whose positive version, (peccable), is rarely or never heard. Others

107

include dishevelled, distraught, unkempt, unfurl and indelible. (see GORMLESS).

INCORRECTLY statistical analysis of speech data shows that this is the word which is most frequently pronounced incorrectly.

INCUNABULA are early books particularly those printed before 1500. It can also mean the cradle or birthplace of a thing. From the Latin *incubabula,* swaddling clothes.

INDICATORY, meaning pointing out or indicative, is an anagram of DICTIONARY.

INDIVISIBILITIES is a sixteen-letter word in which the letter I appears seven times.

INFANT is from the Latin for 'unable to speak'.

INFINITESIMAL immeasurably or incalculably small. Any quantity, no matter how small, can be subdivided into yet smaller portions, or infinitesimals.

INNUENDO an insinuation, an oblique allusion, sometimes of a derogatory or rude nature. From the Latin *innuere*, to nod. When you make an innuendo you give a little nod of the head.

INSIGNIFICANT OTHER a derogatory term for one's spouse.

INTENSE where campers sleep.

INTERCALARY referring to a period of time inserted in the calendar year to make it conform with the solar year e. g. February 29th in a leap year.

INTERNECINE involving mutual slaughter or murder within a group. From the Latin *inter*, between and *necare*, to kill.

INTESTINE comes from the Latin for within. Half the long intestine is a semicolon.

INTROSPECTION If you do not know what this word means then you need to take a long hard look at yourself.

INTRUDER How does an intruder get into a house? Intruder window.

INVALID changes its meaning depending on where the stress is placed. So, inVALid means incorrect; invalID means somebody who is crippled.

IPSEDIXITISM dogmatic assertion. From the Latin *ipse dixit* meaning he (the master) said it. Hence, an assertion made without evidence, resting entirely on the authority of the speaker.

IRREDENTIST originally somebody who believed that all Italian-speaking people should be united politically. A person who advocates the redeeming of territory from another state. Nothing to do with teeth! From the Italian *Italia irredenta*, unredeemed Italy.

J

JADE a precious stone believed to protect its wearers from colic and kidney diseases. Also known as colic stone or nephrite, from *nephros*, Greek for kidney.

JALOPY a battered or decrepit old car. Possibly from Jalapa, Mexico, where many old cars from the USA were sent.

JAMBOREE An international gathering of boy scouts or any large lively party. Probably from the Swahili *Jambo,* meaning hello.

JAZZ the earliest printed uses in 1912 are in California baseball writing, where it meant lively or energetic as in, 'Let's jazz this up!' Soon after it was used to describe a new kind of syncopated music in Chicago.

JEEP said to originate from the letters GP standing for 'General Purpose' vehicle.

JEEPERS CREEPERS a US slang expression of surprise was a euphemism for Jesus Christ.

JENGA is a popular game. The word comes from the Swahili for building.

JENTACULAR relating to breakfast. Something to ponder as you eat your jentacular eggs.

JIGGERY-POKERY trickery or deception. From the Scots *jouk,* to dodge and *pawk,* trick.

JIGSAW a puzzle derived from the name of the tool used to cut it from wood, a kind of fretsaw.

JINGO the word for God in the Basque language. By Jingo!

JITTERBUG an energetic two-step dance or a person who performs it. A forerunner of the jive.

JOANNA rhyming slang for a piano.

JOBSWORTH an unhelpful official who adheres rigidly to petty rules. From the expression, 'It is more than my job's worth to let you…..'

JOKOL an old word used on the Shetland islands to mean yes. It literally means Yes Carl. From the old Norse *jo,* yes *karl,* carl.

JOURNEY comes from the French *journee,* and originally meant the distance you could walk in a day.

JUGGERNAUT a massive force that flattens everything in its path. A heavy truck. The 14th century missionary Friar Odoric brought to Europe the story of an enormous carriage that bore an image of the Hindu god Vishnu, whose title was *Jagannath*, literally, "lord of the world". The story went that some worshippers deliberately allowed themselves to be crushed beneath the vehicle's wheels as a sacrifice to Vishnu.

JUMBO means huge. It comes from the name of a famous elephant named Jumbo who was a popular sight at the London Zoo for 17 years. In 1872 the U.S. showman P.T. Barnum bought the animal for $10,000. Thanks to circus publicity, the name jumbo came to mean unusually large.

A Poster for Jumbo the Elephant

JUNIPER did you bite that woman?

JURY twelve people picked to decide which side has the better lawyer.

JUSSIVE expressing a command. From the Latin *jubere*, to order.

K

KAIZEN is a Japanese term meaning change for the better. It is a business philosophy of continuous improvement.

KAMERAD a German word for 'surrender', often heard in war films. Comrade or friend in German.

KANGAROO an Australian marsupial. It was said that when settlers asked the natives what the animal was called, they replied 'I don't know' which was 'kan ga roo' in their language. But in fact, in the Aborigine language of Guugu Yimidhirr *gangaa roo* does mean kangaroo.

KANGAROO COURT an unfair court which jumps to conclusions.

KARAOKE a Japanese word meaning empty orchestra.

KARMADHARAYA a Sanskrit term for a compound word where the first part describes the second part, such as bluebird or widespread.

KAYAK is a PALINDROME. It comes from the Inuit of Greenland, who called their long boat *qajaq*. Kayak is used by the Innuit people to denote a man's boat. Umaik is their word for a woman's boat.

KERAUNOPHOBIA a morbid fear of thunder and lightning. From the Greek *keraunos*, thunderbolt, and *phobos*, fear. Not to be confused with………..

KERAUNOTHNETOPHOBIA a fear of having a manmade satellite fall from the sky and hit you.

KETCHUP a smooth thick sauce. In the 17th century, the Chinese mixed a concoction of pickled fish and spices and called *itkôe-chiap* or *kê-chiap*. It made its way to the Malay states where it was later discovered by English explorers. That word evolved into the English word ketchup.

KETTLE another name for the common water 'otter.

KICK the curved indentation at the base of a wine bottle. Officially, it is there to add strength to the bottle, but many drinkers suspect it is there to cut down on the amount of wine available. Also called a punt.

KIBOSH comes from the Irish *caip bais* the cap of death, so to put the kibosh on something means to doom it.

KINNIKINICK a mixture used by Native Americans as a substitute for tobacco.

KIOSK a Turkish word for palace. In English it means something much less grand, maybe a stall, telephone box, bandstand or PAVILION.

KISS an acronym used in Marketing for Keep It Simple Stupid.

KNACKER to wear out or exhaust. A knacker was originally someone who bought and slaughtered old horses and worn-out animals – in a knacker's yard.

KNAPSACK a sleeping bag.

KOALA the name of this cuddly animal is derived from an Australian Aborigine word meaning 'no drink'. The koala is believed to be the inspiration for the teddy bear. Koala bears are not bears, they are marsupials.

KODAK a revolutionary and successful form of film processing invented by Charles Eastman in 1892. The word has no specific origin or source. A friend advised him that K was a good letter to use in a name and that five letters was optimal. So he chose Kodak for his company. Sadly, it has become a victim of the digital revolution.

KOWTOW to abase oneself, to grovel or fawn. From an old Chinese custom of touching the forehead to the ground as a sign of deference. From the Chinese *k'o,* knock and *t'ou,* head.

KRAKEN a huge and mythical sea monster. From the Norwegian *kraken*, such a beast.

KRYPTON an element with atomic number 36. It is a rare inert gas sometimes used in fluorescent lights. From the Greek *kryptein* to hide. The Scottish chemist William Ramsay was awarded the 1904 Nobel Prize in Chemistry for the discovery of a series of noble gases, including krypton. Kryptonite is a fictional material that appears in Superman stories. It emits a radiation that weakens Superman but is harmless to humans. Thank goodness.

L

LACTOSE someone who is missing parts of their foot. If this makes them angry they become LACTOSE INTOLERANT.

LACUNA a gap or hiatus from the same word in Latin. In tax avoidance terms a lacuna is better than a loophole as it is a situation where there is no applicable law whereas a loophole is usually the result of a poorly drafted law.

LAMINA a thin plate or layer. The EMORDNILAP for lamina is animal, which leads to this cute PALINDROME - Meet animals, laminate 'em.

LANCASTER capital city of the English county of Lancashire. Any English city or town with name ending in -STER was very probably the site of a Roman camp. *Castra* is the Latin word for camp. Examples are Chester, Doncaster, Gloucester, Leicester, Manchester and Worcester.

LANDLUBBER a seafarer's derogatory term for someone who knows little or nothing of the sea or seamanship.

From the Danish *lobbes*, a clown; not a 'land lover' as is often thought.

LANGUEDOC an area and language in Southern France. It was the place where people said Oc instead of Oui. So it means the language of Oc.

LASER is an acronym for Light Amplification by the Stimulated Emission of Radiation.

LATCHSTRING has six successive consonants, a curious property it shares with CATCHPHRASE.

LATHE a machine which contains both the French and the English definite articles.

LEAD PENCIL there is no lead in a lead pencil. It contains graphite, which is an allotrope of carbon. Two other allotropes of carbon are coal and diamond. Metallic lead will actually leave a trace when rubbed on paper, and maybe this is where the name came from.

LEGO probably the most common toy in the world and the most annoying if you ever step on a piece in the dark. From the Danish *leg godt*, meaning play well.

LEMNISCATE the figure of eight symbol for infinity. It means decorated with ribbons in Latin.

LEPIDOPTERIST someone who studies butterflies and moths. FLUTTER BY is a very apt anagram of BUTTERFLY.

LETHE a river in Hades, the classical underworld, whose water when drunk erased memory of the past. From the Greek *lethe*, oblivion, the ETYMON of lethal.

LIBEL and SLANDER these two words are often confused. Libel is a written statement damaging another's reputation, whereas slander is a false oral statement about another person. Slander is also called calumny.

LIBROCUBICULARIST a person who reads in bed.

A librocubicularist

LIQUORICE (or LICORICE) a black substance used as a medicine or as a flavouring for confectionery. It is extracted from the root of the leguminous plant Glycyrrhiza glabra. Not to be confused with LIQUORISH, which means 'fond of the bottle'.

LIEBFRAUMILCH a German white wine from the Rhine region. It was originally made at a convent dedicated to the Virgin Mary, *Liebfrau*, and *Milch* is milk.

LIMEY an American term for a British sailor who when at sea drank lime juice to prevent scurvy which is caused by a lack of Vitamin C.

LINE from the Latin *linum,* flax from which we also get linen. A line was a thread from a piece of flax. A straight line comes from stretched linen.

LIPOGRAM a composition, often a verse, in which the author deliberately omits one letter or combination of letters. From the Greek *lipein,* to leave and *gramma,* a letter.

LIRP to lirp is to snap your fingers.

LIST and ROLL are remarkable because they are synonyms twice with different meanings. A ship can list or roll and a schedule can be a list or roll.

LISTEN to listen you have to stay SILENT and the two words are anagrams.

LITHIUM from the Greek word for a stone *lithos,* from which we get monolith and megalith. Lithium is the lightest metal and the lightest solid element. It is used in the manufacture of batteries, and its compounds are useful in the treatment of mental illness.

LITORAL connected with the shore. The basis of this rare triple pun; the shore was litorally covered with newspapers.

LITOTES is understatement or affirmation by denial of the contrary. E.g. – a man of no small wealth. LITOTES is an anagram of TOILETS and of T S ELIOT.

LOADSAMONEY a person loaded with wealth because of the Thatcherite economics of the 1980s. Based on a grotesque character invented by comedian Harry Enfield.

LOCUM somebody who fills in for someone else, usually a doctor or dentist. Short for *locum tenens*, Latin for holding a place.

LOGANAMNOSIS the condition of being obsessed with trying to remember forgotten words.

LOGANBERRY a hybrid between a raspberry and a blackberry, first achieved by Judge Logan in California in 1883.

LOGOPHILE a lover of words. However, a LOGOMANIAC is a person who is obsessively interested in words. From the Greek *logos* word, *phileein* to love, *maniakos* madness.

LOONSLATT an obsolete Scottish coin whose value was 13 1/2 pence. The significance of the amount is that it was the usual fee paid to the hangman for carrying out his gruesome task.

LOOSEN and UNLOOSEN mean the same thing.

LOVE why should you never date a tennis player? Because love means nothing to them. The name TENNIS comes from the French *tenez* hold or receive. Many people believe that LOVE stands for zero in tennis because *l'Oeuf* - an egg - looks like a zero but this may be APOCHRYPHAL.

LOVE APPLE is an old name for a tomato, believed by some to be the apple Eve gave to Adam.

LUCRE meaning money or profit is often used in a derogatory way e.g., in the phrase filthy lucre. From the Latin *lucrum*, profit, from which we also get lucrative.

LUDO is a game named after the Latin, *ludo*, I play.

LYCANTHROPE a werewolf.

M

MAE WEST was a popular name for a naval inflatable life jacket. It was named after the buxom U.S. film star Mae West (1892-1980).

MAGIC from the Middle English *magik*, from old French *magique*, from Latin *magicus*, from Greek *magikos*, from Old Persian *magush* sorcerer.

MAGICIAN what do you call a magician who has lost his magic? Ian.

MAGPIE mag is short for Margaret and was an old derogatory term for an idle or chattering woman. Pie is the French word for the bird. So, a chattering bird.

MARRIED is an anagram of ADMIRER.

MALAPROPISM the misapplication of words of similar sound. The word comes from a character named Mrs. Malaprop in Sheridan's 1775 play The Rivals. E.g. she refers to an allegory on the banks of the Nile. Malapropos means out of place or unsuitable.

MALARIA is derived from Italian words *mal aria*, meaning 'bad air'. This was the basis of the miasma theory which held that disease was caused by foul odours emanating from swamps. The ancient Romans controlled malaria by draining the swamps, little realising that what they were doing was destroying the habitat of mosquitoes, the real culprits. Malaria is one of the principal causes of premature death on our planet today.

MALARKEY absurd talk, nonsense. American slang. Also, an Irish surname.

MALTA the name is derived from the Greek word *meli*, honey. The ancient Greeks called the island *Melitē* meaning honey-sweet. An endemic subspecies of bees live on the island and produce excellent honey.

MALAYALAM is a language spoken in the Kerala region of India. The word is a nine-letter palindrome.

MALI is a country in West Africa. The name means the place where the king lives. MALI is the only country name, which is an anagram of another country's capital, LIMA, the capital of Peru. (But see TOBAGO).

MAMELUKE a former member of the ruling class in Egypt. Originally Caucasian slaves who seized power in 13th century. Also, a white slave in a Muslim country. From the Arabic *malaka*, to possess.

MANDARIN a Chinese official, the official language of China, any high-ranking official or bureaucrat. A small orange named for its resemblance of its colour to that of robes worn by mandarins. From the Portuguese *mandarim*, from the Sanskrit *mantra*, counsel.

MANGELWURZEL a type of beet used as food for cattle. From the German *mangold*, beet and *wurzel*, root.

MANTELPIECE a shelf over a fireplace on which ornaments, or framed family photographs are displayed. It gets its name from the fact that people used to hang their cloaks or mantles over the fireplace to dry them.

MANTRA a Hindu sacred text, a chanted or repeated meditation. Sanskrit *mantra*, charm or counsel.

MARGARINE a substitute for butter whose name is derived from the Greek word *margarites* meaning pearl. This is also the source of the name Margaret.

MARCH is one of only three months which have anagrams. MARCH has CHARM, APRIL has PILAR and MAY has YAM.

MARGHERITA the margherita pizza was made for Queen Margherita, wife of King Umberto of Italy on their visit to Naples in the 1889.   It was designed to show the red, white and green of the Italian flag by the use of tomatoes, mozzarella and herbs.

MARIJUANA is a Mexican rendering of the name Mary Jane.   Pot comes from the Mexican Spanish word *potiguaya* meaning marijuana.

MARS and MURRIE the original inventors of M & M chocolates in 1941 called their product after their own initials.

MARTINGALE has two meanings. The first is a strap fastened to the noseband and girth of a horse to prevent it from rearing. The second meaning is a gambling system where the stakes are doubled after each loss. Don't try it. It works in theory but most casinos have an upper limit which stops this succeeding.

MATRIX an array, especially a mathematical one consisting of rows and columns, containing symbols. Originally a womb or uterus. From the Latin *mater*, mother.

MAUSOLEUM a large burial chamber is named after Mausolus, a Greek Emperor of the 4th century BC. His Mausoleum at Halicarnassus was one of the Seven Wonders of the Ancient World.

MAVERICK one who does not conform. From Samuel Maverick (1803--1870), a Texan cattle owner who refused to brand his cattle.

MAYDAY this internationally understood distress call has nothing to do with a day in May. It comes from the French *m'aidez* which means 'help me'. Similarly, SOS does not stand for any particular word. It comes from morse code (three dots, three dashes, three dots) a very easy message to transmit in times of extreme distress.

McGUFFIN an object that is necessary to the plot of a book or film but is insignificant in itself. It was devised by Angus MacPhail for films but was brought to perfection by the great director, Alfred Hitchcock.

ME is the commonest Latin word in use today.

MEDITERRANEAN means situated in the middle of the earth.

MELBA Dame Nellie Melba (1861--1931), the great Australian soprano, was born Helen Mitchell, but changed her name to Melba after her native city of Melbourne. She has two foodstuffs named after her. The first is Toast Melba, very thinly sliced and overdone toasted bread, served to her by mistake in a London hotel. The second is Peach Melba, consisting of peaches, ice cream and raspberry sauce, created in her honour by a French chef.

MELLIFLUOUS sweet as if flowing with honey. From the Latin *mel*, honey, and *fluere*, to flow. *Fluere* is also the source of fluent.

MEMENTO a keepsake. From the Latin verb *meminisse* to remember. The first words of Psalm 131 as said in the Latin Mass are *Memento Domine* meaning Remember Lord.

MENDACITY and MENDICITY are often confused. Mendacity is the practice of lying, while mendicity is the act of begging or living on alms.

MERCURY is the only metal which is liquid at room temperature. It shares its name with a planet and the messenger of the Gods.

MERKIN a pubic wig. In the 17th century women would sometimes shave their pubic area to get rid of lice, and then wear a merkin.

MESMERIZE to bedazzle, enthral, or hypnotize. From the eponymous French doctor Franz Mesmer (1734-1815) who was either a quack or a genius. He gained fame by treating patients with a force he termed animal magnetism but which was probably hypnotism.

MESS a place where military personnel dine - but usually well-kept and tidy! The root is the Old French *mes*, portion of food.

METRONOME a dwarf who lives in the Paris Underground.

MEXICO is a six-letter country name which contains eight numbers: M, X, XI, IC, C, O, the irrational number e and the imaginary number i.

MILKOMEDA the Andromeda Galaxy is approaching the Milky Way at about 110 kilometres per second (68 miles per second). They will collide in approximately 4.5 billion years and form a new galaxy whose name is Milkomeda.

MIRANDIZE to read the legal rights to a suspect arrested on a criminal charge. From Ernesto Miranda (1941-1976), a labourer whose conviction on kidnapping, rape, and armed robbery was overturned because arresting officers had failed to inform him of his legal rights. At age 34, he was stabbed to death in a bar fight. The man suspected of killing him invoked his Miranda rights and refused to talk to police. He was released and never charged with Miranda's murder.

MITHRIDATISM immunity against poisons produced by gradually increasing small doses of the poison itself. Practiced by Mithridates, King of Pontus around 60 BC, who made himself immune in this way.

MNEMONIC starts with a silent M. It comes from the Greek *mneme* - memory. A mnemonic is a device to aid the memory. E.g. Man very early made jars stand up nearly perpendicularly – helps you remember the order of the planets going out from the Sun. Mercury, Venus, Earth Mars, Jupiter, Saturn, Uranus, Neptune and Pluto. Here is another to help you spell mnemonic - Memorisation's Never Easy; Memory Often Needs Initial Cues.

MOLLBUZZER a pickpocket whose victims are women.

MONDAY is the only day of the week with a single word anagram, DYNAMO.

MONDEGREEN a misheard phrase in a poem or a song. An example is 'Gladly the cross I'd bear ' being heard as 'Gladly the cross-eyed bear'. The word comes from a Scottish poem with the lines; They have slain the Earl of Moray and laid him on the green. The second line was rendered as; 'And Lady Mondegreen' - a non-existent woman.

MONKEY'S WEDDING a South African expression for simultaneous rain and sunshine.

MOONBOW a rainbow that happens at night. They are rare and can appear near mist or a waterfall when there is a full moon.

MOUNTEBANK someone who supplies worthless potions, pills , and fake medicines. A lovely alternative word to quack and charlatan. From Italian *montare,* to mount *banco,* bench.

MONTH a time period originally based on the time it took for the MOON to go around the Earth. Both words come from the same ancient root German *mond* and Greek *men*. Month is one of those rare words with no rhyme in English (see ORANGE).

MOUNTWEAZEL a non-existent word, person, or country inserted deliberately in a dictionary, biography, or atlas to expose plagiarists. The source of the term is the fictitious Lillian Mountweazel, a bogus entry in the fourth edition of The New Columbia Encyclopaedia in 1975. Think upon it—any word here may be a mountweazel inserted in this book to trap you!

MOPED a small motorcycle with pedals. The word was created by the Swedish journalist Harald Nielsen in 1952, as a portmanteau of the Swedish words *motor* and *pedaler.*

MORTSAFE a heavy metal grating used to guard a corpse against RESURRECTIONISTS.

MOTHEATEN moths are much maligned. These insects do not in fact eat clothes. It is their larvae which do the damage.

MOTHER the words for mother sound very similar in nearly all languages and almost always begin with the letter M.

MOUSE the first computer mouse was known as an x-y position indicator. The plural of the computer mouse is mouses.

MOZAMBIQUE is the only single-word country name containing all five vowels.

MULLIGAN a golfing term for a free stroke after a poor shot. Hence any short pardon. An EPONYM from Canadian golfer, Charles Mulligan, whose friends in the 1920s gave him an extra shot in gratitude for driving them to their golf club in Montreal.

MUMBO-JUMBO meaning nonsense or empty talk is a Mandingo word for an ancient idol. The Mandingo language is spoken by the Mandinka people in parts of Guinea, Senegal, and The Gambia.

MUMPSIMUS a view or opinion stubbornly held even when shown to be wrong. The story is that an ignorant priest repeatedly said mumpsimus when he should have said sumpsimus during the Latin Mass.

MURMURATION a collective name for starlings. Such a flock can produce striking patterns in flight.

MURPHY a potato, because of its connection with Ireland, where Murphy is the most common surname.

MID the word which is the largest number when viewed as Roman Numerals – 1499.

MISANDRY a hatred of men; a counterpart to misogyny, a hatred of women.

MORTGAGE is literally a death-pledge from the Latin *mortus,* dead (from which we get mortal and mortality).

MURDER a collective name for a group of crows.

MUZAK bland music piped into offices, elevators and shops. Said to have been inspired by music and Kodak.

NAMES Men's first names tend to have fewer syllables than women's first names. And in a man's name, the stress is generally on the first syllable, while it is usually on the second syllable in a woman's name.

NASOPHARYNGITIS the medical name for the common cold.

NAUGHTY in the Middle Ages someone who was naughty was very poor, someone who had naught.

NEANDERTHAL an extinct hominid that lived in Europe, Africa and Asia from about 30,000 to 200,000 years ago. Named after *Neanderthal*, Neander Valley in Germany where remains were found in 1856. Ironically, *Neander* means new man.

NEATNIK slang for a tidy, well-groomed person, as distinct from a beatnik.

NECKTIE PARTY nineteenth century black humour for a hanging.

NECROMANCY foretelling the future using corpses or the spirits of the dead. From the Greek *neckros*, a corpse. The Roman equivalent was auspices, using the entrails of birds.

NEPHROID is a kidney shape such as the curve seen on the top of your cup on a sunny morning.

NERD the word was invented by Dr Seuss and first appeared in his 1950 book *If I Ran the Zoo*.

NIBLICK a lovely old word for a golf club. It was the equivalent of a modern 9 iron. A mashie was the equivalent of a 5 iron. And a mashie niblick was something in between - maybe a modern 7 iron.

NICE originally meant ignorant, foolish, or unaware. It comes from the Latin *ne* not and *scire* to know. Over the centuries this word has had a remarkable number of different meanings in common usage moving from wanton to coy to timid to fussy to delicate to precise to agreeable.

NICKEL Copper miners in Germany often found an ore which looked promising but yielded no copper. They believed that the devil, Old Nick, was trying to fool them, so they called the ore KUPFERNICKEL, Copper Nickel. But Nickel turned out to be an important chemical element with many uses in industry.

NICOTINE is named after Jean Nicot, the French ambassador to Portugal, who brought tobacco plants to France from a trip to Portugal in 1559. Nicotine from tobacco was at first believed to have medicinal properties but is now seen as a poison.

NICTITATE to wink or blink. From the Latin *nictare*, to blink. Scientists use the term nictitating membrane to describe the thin, transparent membrane in the eyes of some birds and reptiles that keeps the eyeball moist and clean.

NIGGARD a person who begrudges spending money, a miser. Used by Shakespeare but risky to use nowadays as it might be misheard.

NIMBY a person who opposes something unpleasant in the area where they live, while raising no such objections if it happens elsewhere. An acronym standing for Not In My Back Yard. An extreme NIMBY can become a BANANA – Build Absolutely Nothing Anywhere Near Anyone.

NINCOMPOOP a simpleton, an idiot, a stupid person. Probably from the Latin *non compos mentis* not in possession of one's wits.

NINTENDO is a major Japanese company founded in 1889 to make playing cards. The name means 'Leave luck to heaven.'

NITWIT a stupid person--somebody with the brains of a nit or a head louse.

NOCTAMBULIST a sleepwalker. A synonym for a somnambulist. One comes from the root of night and the other from sleep.

NOGGIN originally a mug or cup but now someone's head.

NONCHALANT indifferent, unconcerned, cool. Originally from the Latin *non,* not *calere,* to be hot.

NONNY-NONNY a refrain, often used in folk songs to cover up rude words.

NONPLUSSED its actual meaning is so taken aback by something that you are left speechless. However, its modern usage is the exactly the opposite - apathetic about something.

It is NOTABLE that sometimes you are NOT ABLE to see NO TABLE.

NUDIUSTERTIAN means relating to the day before yesterday. From the Latin *nudius tertius,* now is the third day.

NULLABOR a plain in South-Eastern Australia. It is a flat arid desert of limestone bedrock covering 200,000 square kilometres. It contains virtually no trees. Its name is from the Latin *null arbor,* no tree. A bad place to walk your dog.

NULLO is extreme body modification mostly by men who choose to have their genitals, nipples or toes surgically removed. Nullo is a contraction of genital nullification.

NUTARIAN a vegetarian who lives mostly on nuts.

NUTS IN MAY an old children's rhyme has the line 'Here we go gathering nuts in May'. But there are no nuts on the trees in May (unless you live in the southern hemisphere). Nuts is probably a corruption of knots of flowers, collected in May to be laid on religious shrines.

NYLON a synthetic polymer, a stocking made of this material. The name was coined by the Dupont Company who invented nylon in 1939. The persistent idea that it is an acronym for New York and London is a myth.

O

OASIS a fertile spot in the desert, is the same word in French, Latin and Greek. It comes from the ancient Egyptian word *wehe*, a vessel in the sand.

OBLOQUY is censure, calumny, heavy criticism or disgrace. From the Latin *ob loqui,* to speak against.

OBSTETRIC relating to childbirth. It literally means 'someone who stands in the way' of a woman giving birth. From the Latin *obstare*, to stand opposite. Obstacle has the same root.

OCKHAM'S RAZOR a philosophical principle which implies that explanations which are as simple as possible are the most likely to be true. It is called after the English Franciscan monk William of Ockham (1285-1349), a pupil of Duns Scotus, who is believed to have first formulated it.

OCTOTHORPE the name for the symbol # on the keyboard. Sometimes called hash. It has been given a new lease of life by modern social media and the hashtag. Octo is from the Latin for eight and the octothorpe has eight legs. No-one is quite sure where the thorpe comes from.

ODD it is odd that NEVER ODD OR EVEN is a palindrome.

ODIOUS hateful. From the Latin *odium*, hate. Unconnected with ODOROUS which means fragrant and MALODOROUS - smelly.

OK is the abbreviation which is most understood around the world by people who do not speak English.

OMBUDSMAN an official (man or woman) who is charged with representing the interests of the public by investigating and addressing complaints. The word comes from the Swedish *ombudsman* which comes from the Old Norse *umbodsmaor* meaning proxy or representative.

OMBRIFUGE anything that provides protection from the rain, e.g. an awning or an umbrella. From the Greek *ombro,* rain and *fuge,* repelling.

An ombrifuge in action

ONE is the only number whose letters are in reverse alphabetical order.

ONOMATOPOEIA a figure of speech where the sound of a word echoes its meaning. Examples are plop and fizzy. Widely used in poetry. From the Greek *onomatopoiia*, word-making.

OPOSSUM the only North American marsupial gets its name from the native American Powhatan language where it means white dog. Skunk, coyote, raccoon, moose, woodchuck, and caribou are other animals whose names come from native American tongues.

ORANGE There are no words which rhyme with orange, diamond, ninth, pint, purple, silver or month.

ORCHID the name of this plant comes from the Greek *orkhis*, literally meaning testicle, because of the shape of the root.

ORDEAL a sale at the paddle shop.

ORIGINAL WORDS the person who has contributed the most original words to the English language is Geoffrey Chaucer (1342-1400). His 1900 contributions include bagpipe, government, and twitter. The runner up is William Shakespeare, who gave us critic, hunchback, and barefaced, as well as over seven hundred other words.

OSCAR the only Oscar to win an Oscar was Oscar Hammerstein II for best song in 1941 and 1945.

OSTRACISE the Ancient Greeks had a procedure for banishing for between five and ten years someone suspected likely to subvert the state. They wrote his name on a piece of pottery before placing it in an urn. From the Greek *Ostrakon,* a potshard.

OTIOSE futile, superfluous, redundant. From the Latin *otiosus*, at leisure.

OUAGADOUGOU is the capital of the African republic of Burkina Faso (whose name means – Land of the Honest Men.) Ouagadougou is the only city we know which starts with three vowels and the only city with eight vowels and just three consonants.

OUGH has the most different pronunciations in English. Among these are; rough, trough, hiccough, bough, cough, through and thorough.

OUT OF BOUNDS an exhausted kangaroo.

OVULAR means relating to an ovule, the body containing the egg cell. The word has been used by extreme feminists to replace the masculine overtones of SEMINAR. From the Latin *ovum* egg.

OVUM the largest cell in the human body. The male spermatozoon is the smallest. One up for the girls!

OX unusual in that its plural, OXEN, is twice as long. Similarly, IT and HE, which become THEY in the plural.

OXYMORON where two contradictory words or ideas are juxtaposed. E.g. less is more, deafening silence, or passive aggressive. From the Greek *oxys* sharp and *moros* foolish.

OXYPHENBUTAZONE an anti-inflammatory medication used to treat arthritis. This 15-letter word is supposedly the highest-possible scoring word in Scrabble play. As far as we know it has never been played and maybe never will. If the right letters are already in place, then it can theoretically be played across three triple word score squares for a score of 1778.

PACHYDERM A lovely word for an elephant, a rhinoceros, or a hippopotamus. It can also refer to a hard-bitten person as it literally means having a thick skin. From the Greek *pachys*, thick and *derma*, skin.

PAINTER a strong rope used to anchor a boat. From Latin *pendere*, to hang.

PAJAMA or PYJAMA comes from the Hindi word, *pajama*, which itself comes from combining the Persian words for leg and garment.

PAKISTAN is an acronym. The name was coined 14 years before the country gained independence by Choudhary Rahmat Ali. He advocated the creation of a state comprising the 30 million Muslims in five northern regions of India: Punjab, Afghan province, Kashmir, Sind and Baluchistan. He combined the first letter of the first four regions and the ending of Baluchistan, to make PAKSTAN (he added an i in the middle to help pronunciation). Also, Pakistan means 'land of the pure' in Urdu.

PALACE comes from the Latin *Palatium*, the Roman emperor's residence on the Palatine hill in Rome.

PALAVER originally, a discussion between traders and natives particularly African tribespeople. Nowadays, just silly talk. From the Portuguese *palavra* word.

PALIMPSEST an ancient manuscript in which the original writing has been written over, perhaps several times. From the Greek *palimpsestos* - scraped again.

PALINDROME a word, verse or sentence that reads the same backward and forward. E.g. Live dirt up a side track carted is a putrid evil.

PANACHE originally a plume of feathers. Now a confident manner or swagger.

PANDEMONIUM where all the devils and demons live. A word coined by the poet John Milton to describe Hell in his work Paradise Lost. It has come to mean uproar and utter confusion. From the Greek *pan* all and *daimon* spirit.

PANGLOSSIAN means taking an excessively optimistic view of the world as did Dr Pangloss in Voltaire's *Candide*.

PANGRAM a sentence which contains every letter of the alphabet. E.g. The quick brown fox jumps over a lazy dog.

PANIC comes from fear of the Greek God of the woods, Pan. He had the childish habit of jumping out from behind trees to frighten people and causing them to panic.

PANOPLY a brilliant covering or array comes from the from Greek *panoplia,* a complete suit of armour.

PANOPTICON a circular prison where the guards could at all times keep an eye on their prisoners. A word invented by English philosopher, Jeremy Bentham, from the Greek *panoptos*, fully visible.

PANSY a pretty flower, from the French *pensee*, a thought, as the flowers have a pensive look about them.

PANTRY a larder or small room where food is stored. From French *paneterie* bread room, from Latin *panis* bread.

PANTS comes to us from the Italian word pantaloons which were baggy trousers named after travelling actors from Venice who wore them. Venetians were called *pantaloni* because their patron saint was the Roman martyr St Pantaleon.

PAPER comes from the ancient Egyptian plant papyrus which was used to make a material for writing.

PARADIGM originally meaning a perfect example of its type, but now used more to mean a theoretical framework. From the Greek *paradeigma*, an example.

PARADOX a self-contradictory statement or something which is apparently absurd, but which may be true. Alternatively, a paradox is two physicians.

PARANESIA I am sure I have seen this word before. It is the medical term for déjà vu.

PARAPHERNALIA what was left of the bride's possessions after her dowry had been paid to her husband. Later it came to mean just baggage. From the Greek *para*, beside, and *pherne*, fortune.

PARASITE comes from the Greek *para* alongside and *sitos* bread. It means someone eating alongside you at the table. However, some people think that parasites are what you see from the Eiffel Tower.

PARLIAMENT a representative assembly, from the French *parler*, to speak. Also, a collective name for owls.

PAS DE DEUX French for father of twins.

PASS when you pass an examination, you take a step forward to the next level. *Passus* is the Latin for a step.

PASSION originally suffering, as in the passion of Christ. From the Latin, *passum*, to suffer. Later it came to mean love and extreme feeling.

PATER NOSTER Our Father in Latin is the opening of the Lord's Prayer. It also means anything strung like a rosary such as hooks on a fishing line or small lakes connected by rivers. It also refers to an elevator which stops and opens automatically at every floor, so that it can be used by Orthodox Jewish people on the sabbath, when even pressing a lift button is regarded as work.

PATINA a thin layer that forms on the surface of certain metals such as copper, bronze, or brass, usually as a result of oxidation. The word is also used for the sheen on wooden furniture and is a major factor in the value of antiques. It comes from a Latin word meaning 'shallow dish', where presumably it was first noticed.

PATTER nonsensical chatter. Believed to be derived from the Lord's Prayer, the Our Father or PATER NOSTER, spoken by people who did not understand Latin.

PAVILION a large tent or canopy. The word comes from the Latin *papilio*, butterfly, because the flaps of a pavilion resembled the wings of the insect.

PECULIAR distinctive, odd or uncommon. Originally - belonging exclusively to one person. Literally "property in cattle". From the Latin *pecus* cattle, and one's private property.

PEG'S LAW a MNEMONIC for remembering the seven deadly sins; Pride, Envy, Gluttony, Sloth Lust, Avarice and Wrath.

PELAGIC oceanic, pertaining to the open sea and the fish found therein. From the Greek *pelagos*, sea.

PERCENTAGE the % sign is a jumbled-up version of one hundred, 100.

PERESTROIKA rebuilding and reform. One of the few Russian words to have made it into mainstream English. It is associated with Mikhail Gorbachev who introduced sweeping changes in the Soviet Union.

PERIPATETIC relating to Aristotle's school of philosophy, who taught while *peripatetikos* or walking about, at the Lyceum in Athens. It now means wandering or moving from place to place.

PERMIT is both a noun and a verb. The noun is pronounced with the emphasis on the first syllable, while the verb is pronounced with the emphasis on the second syllable. There are many other noun-verbs where this applies, for example produce, contact and contract.

PETERMAN a thief who breaks into and robs safes.

PETREL a seagull which flies close to the surface of the sea which it touches with its feet. It is named after Saint Peter who reputedly walked on water as reported in Saint Matthew's Gospel.

PETRICHOR the pleasant odour of rain on warm ground.

PETTIFOGGER a lawyer whose methods are petty, underhanded, or disreputable.

PHANEROMANIA an irresistible desire to pick at a scab or bite one's nails.

PHANTASMAGORICAL full of diverse or terrifying images, like something in a confused dream. From the Greek *phantasma,* image or phantom.

PHARMACIST a helper on a farm.

PHILOCALIST a lover of beautiful things. An admirer of the PULCHRITUDINOUS.

PHLOGISTON a substance now known not to exist, postulated by early chemists as escaping from a body when it was burned. From the Greek *phlogistos*, burnt.

PIANO is a contraction of pianoforte which literally means soft-loud in Italian. The ability to vary the volume was the chief change from its forerunner, the harpsichord.

PICTS an ancient Scottish tribe so-called because they were painted. From the Latin *pingere,* to paint.

PIDGIN a language in which people can communicate if they do not speak the same language. It comes from Pidgin English a corruption of 'Business English', used in the Far East in the nineteenth century.

PINCHFART a miser.

PIPSQUEAK soldier's lang in World War I for a small German shell which made both a pip and a squeak when in flight. Now a name given to an insignificant little fellow.

PISMIRE an archaic word for an ant. It is probably derived from the smell of an ant-heap.

PLACEBO is a Latin word meaning I will please. A placebo was originally a medication designed to please rather than heal. Now it is an inert substance used in medical trials.

PLACENTA the human afterbirth is a Latin word meaning a flat cake, because of its shape.

PLAGIARISM comes from the Latin *plagiarius* – a kidnapper. So a plagiarist is someone who kidnaps other people's ideas.

PLATEAU'S SPHERULE when a water drop falls, it is followed by a minute droplet called Plateau's Spherule. This is named after the Belgian physicist, Joseph Plateau, who also studied the properties of soap bubbles.

PLEB a colloquial term for a common or vulgar lower-class person, especially someone who does not appreciate culture or the arts. In Roman times the Plebeians were commoners looked down on by the Patricians who were the upper classes.

PLETHORA a word that means a lot to me.

PLIMSOLL LINE a marking on the side of a ship below which it must not be submerged for safety reasons. Named after Samuel Plimsoll who introduced many improvements in shipping. Also, a plimsoll is a name for shoes worn on deck.

PNEUMONOULTRAMICROSCOPICSILICOVOLCANOCONIO SIS a disease caused by microscopic volcanic dust. With 45 letters, it is the longest word in the dictionary. Some would contend that it is an artificial word created to win the record. The longest words in common use today are probably counterrevolutionaries with 22 letters (but spelt with a hyphen in some dictionaries) and incomprehensibilities (21 letters). A longer word that is still in most dictionaries is antidisestablishmentarianism (28).

POINTLESS how a triangle would describe a circle.

PONCHO comes from the Araucanian language of the natives of Chile who called their woollen shawl a *pontho*.

PONY EXPRESS the pony express was a mail service delivering messages and mail using relays of riders between Missouri and California. It had no ponies - just horses.

POLARIZE what penguins see through.

POLYSYLLABIC with five syllables is polysyllabic.

PONZI a Ponzi scheme is a financial scam in which early investors are paid off from the contributions of later ones. It is named after the Italian swindler Charles Ponzi who operated this type of con in Boston in 1920.

POOTER a small bottle used by entomologists for collecting insects and little bugs. But the main claim to fame of the word is that it was the surname of Charles Pooter, the anti-hero of Diary of a Nobody, written by George and Weedon Grossmith, a classic of understated humour, published in London in 1892. Pooterish means conventional and unimaginative.

POPPYCOCK nonsense or rubbish. Derived from the Dutch *pappekak* meaning soft dung.

PORCELATOR the little opening in the hand basin or bath that lets water out instead of flooding the room.

POROUS we believe this is the longest word you can make from capital letters containing curved parts.

PORNOCRACY government by prostitutes or by corrupt officials who metaphorically prostitute themselves for power.

PORTMANTEAU a word formed by putting together parts of two other words. E.g. 'brunch', a combination of breakfast and lunch. A more recent example is Brexit. The concept is believed to have been invented by the mathematician Lewis Carroll who wrote Alice in Wonderland. A portmanteau is a large travelling-bag from the French *porter* to carry and *manteau* a cloak.

POSH stylish, top-class, expensive. Supposedly an acronym for Port Out, Starboard Home. On ocean voyages between Britain and India, the most desirable cabins, the ones that didn't get the afternoon heat, were on the port side out and on the starboard side home. These luxury tickets were supposedly stamped with the letters POSH. This is an appealing story but sadly there is no evidence to support it.

POSTPARTUM relating to the time after childbirth. From the Latin *post* after and *parere* to give birth.

POWWOW a conference. From the Alonquian, a priest or a dreamer.

PREFACE an introduction e.g., to a book or to the Mass. The preface of a book is written by the author; the foreword is written by someone else. From the Latin *prae*, before and *fari*, to speak.

PREHENSILE adapted to gripping. Like a monkey's tail or an elephant's trunk. From the Latin *prehendere*, to grasp, from which root we also get comprehend and apprehend.

PREPOSITION a word you are forbidden to end a sentence with.

PRESBYTERIANS is an anagram for BRITNEY SPEARS.

PRESENTS your presents is what is requested of you at a wedding.

PRICKET a spike for a candle; first you must prick the candle.

PRIEST a wooden hammer or a heavy cudgel designed to finish off a fish you have caught. The priest connection is that it is delivering the last rites.

PRIG an insufferable sanctimonious pedant who seeks unnecessary precision in everything.

PRINCES is a plural word which becomes singular when you add an S, princess.

PROBABLE originally meant true, provable by experiment, from the Latin *probare* to prove.

PROCRUSTEAN attempting to produce uniformity and regularity by violent means. It is called after an ancient Greek psychopath, Procrustes, who tied his victims to a bed and attempted to fit them to the bed, stretching them if they were too short, and amputating their limbs if they were too long.

PROPANE a masochist.

PROPINQUITY nearness or proximity. From the Latin *propinquus*, near.

PROPRIETORY belonging to the legal owner. A word that can be formed with the top row of letters on the keyboard. See TYPEWRITER and RUPTUREWORT.

PRUNES are sometimes called black coated workers because of their laxative properties.

PSYCHOKINESIS the ability to move objects with the mind alone without using physical means. A very doubtful possibility.

PULCHRITUDINOUS a beautiful word meaning beautiful. From Latin *pulchritudo*, beauty or excellence.

PUNISHMENT is an anagram of NINE THUMPS.

PURPLE PATCH its true meaning is an overwritten and flowery piece of prose, but it is used by many journalists in an opposite sense - a particularly fine passage of writing or sporting performance.

PSEPHOLOGY the study of voting and voting patterns. From the Greek *psephos*, a pebble. Votes were originally cast by placing pebbles in an urn.

PSEUDOMETRIC in mathematics, a pseudometric space is a generalization of a metric space in which the distance between two distinct points can be zero. The word is of interest because it has an anagram – COMPUTERISED.

PSYCHE the Greek word for butterfly. Many ancient peoples believed that the butterfly represented the human soul freed from its mortal body.

PSYCHOCERAMIC a crackpot.

PSYCHOPOMP a conductor of souls to the other world. From the Greek *psyche* soul and *pompos* guide.

PTARMIGAN a grouse-like bird found in Scotland. From the Gaelic tarmachan. One of the very few words in English that begin with PT.

PTERODACTYL a large flying reptile from the Jurassic period. It had a large skull, long jaws and a flying membrane attached to a long digit on its forelimb. The word comes from the Greek *pteron* wing and *daktylos* finger. Incidentally, you cannot hear a pterodactyl when it goes to the toilet because the p is silent.

PUDENDOUS means shameful. It comes from the Latin *pudere* to make or be ashamed. It is one of only five common words which end in DOUS. The others are stupendous, horrendous, tremendous and hazardous.

PUMPERNICKEL a coarse dark rye bread. Originally a German term of abuse meaning farty Nick. From German *pumpern* to break wind and *Nickel* a goblin or rascal. Possibly then applied to the bread because it made you fart.

PUNDIT an expert authority or commentator. Pundit is Hindi for wise man.

PYRRHIC a type of victory that is not worth winning because so much is lost to achieve it. Named after Pyrrhus, a king of Epirus, who suffered heavy losses in defeating the Romans at Asculum in Apulia in 279 B.C.E.

Q

QANAT an underground channel used to carry water, first used in Iran around 2000 BC. Originally a Persian word, now one of just a handful of words in English where Q is not followed by U.

QANTAS the Australian national airline is an acronym for Queensland And Northern Territory Aerial Service.

QATAR is the only country that begins with the letter Q and IRAQ is the only country that ends with the letter Q.

QUACK calling a doctor by this derogatory name comes from a 19th century Dutch word *quacksalver*, meaning a seller of medicines.

QUALTAGH the first person you see when you leave the house. From Manx, spoken in the Isle of Man.

QUANGO a Quasi-Autonomous Non-Governmental Organisation.

QUARK a word coined by James Joyce in his 1939 book Finnegans Wake. In 1964 U.S. physicist Murray Gell-Mann used it to describe a fundamental subatomic particle. There are six types, known as flavours, of quarks: up, down, strange, charm, bottom, and top.

QUARANTINE a period of isolation or detention to prevent the spread of an infection or contagious disease. It was originally 40 days for a ship which might be carrying a disease. The word comes from the Italian *quaranta* and the Latin *quadraginta* for 40.

QUARTER-POUNDER a piece of cooked minced beef sold in a fast-food outlet. It usually weighs less than one sixth of a pound.

QUEEN would probably be the first word in the dictionary if our alphabet was ordered to match the QWERTY keyboard layout.

QUEUE is just a single letter with several other letters waiting in line behind it.

QUIDNUNC a person who gossips, a newsmonger. From Latin words meaning 'what now?'

QUINCUNX an arrangement of five points or objects at the corners and centre of a square. Often seen with cards, dice or trees. From the Latin *quinque,* five. This word scores heavily in Scrabble.

QUISLING a traitor who sides with the enemy. It comes from Vidkun Quisling (1887-1945), a Norwegian who collaborated with the Nazis during World War 2. He was executed in 1945.

QUIXOTIC in the manner of Cervantes' hero Don Quixote who tilted at windmills thinking they were dangerous giants. By association, extravagantly dotty if well-meaning behaviour.

QUIZZIFY to quiz or question. Scrabble's top 8 letter word. If you draw a Q and a Z and a blank tile (for the second Z) then you can score 419 points.

QUOTIDIAN commonplace, occurring every day. A lovely word for something ordinary.

RADAR an acronym for radio detection and ranging. Since it involves a reflected signal it is very appropriate that RADAR is a PALINDROME.

RAMPANT a term from heraldry. Originally it referred to an animal, typically a lion, standing on its hind legs. The current meaning is excessive or out of control.

RANARIUM a place where frogs are kept, from the Latin *rana*, a frog.

RANSACK to plunder or pillage comes from the Old Norse word *rannsaka,* which means to search a house.

RASE to erase, to demolish, to lay a building level with the ground. So, the exact opposite of its homonym, raise. Rase come from the French *raser* to scrape or cut down from which we also get razor.

RAZZAMATAZZ a HULLABALOO, a razzle-dazzle. Perhaps a varied repetition of JAZZ.

REBARBATIVE means repellent. It comes from the French *barbe*, beard. There is an old French expression *se rebarber* meaning to face each other 'beard to beard' i.e. aggressively.

RECANT comes from Latin; *re*, again, and *cantare* meaning to sing. So literally it means to sing again or, to change your tune.

RECTUM the anus. From the Latin *intestinum rectum*, straight intestine, in contrast to the convolution of the rest of the bowels.

REDNECK a derogatory term for a poor unsophisticated white person drawn from the fact that the back of a labourer's neck is often burnt red by the sun.

REDIVIDER and ROTOVATOR are both nine-letter palindromes.

REGARDANT means looking backwards or over your shoulder. A term from heraldry.

RELATIVITY Einstein's theory that time passes more slowly when you are with your relatives.

RELIEF what trees do in the Spring.

REPERCUSSION a consequence of playing the drums.

RESTAURANT originally a food or place that refreshes or restores you. From the French *restorer*, to restore.

RESURRECTIONIST a polite name for a body-snatcher.

REVENANT someone who returns after a long absence or even death. From the French *revenir*, to return. The name of a 2015 film starring Leonardo DiCaprio.

REVERSE and OBVERSE are the opposite sides of a coin.

RHODE ISLAND is the smallest of the US states, but it is the state with the longest name - State of Rhode Island and Providence Plantations.

RICKSHAW a small two-wheeled carriage drawn by a man. From the Japanese *jinricksha, jin* man, *riki* power, *sha* carriage.

RIPARIAN referring to the bank of a river. Someone who lives by a river. From the Latin *ripa*, a bank.

RIPSNORTER something of exceptional strength. Fast and furious. Often applied to a very fast ball in cricket.

ROBOT is the only Czech word in common use in English. From Karel Capek's play R.U.R. in 1920.

ROMANIA contains another country Oman, as does Somalia with Mali, The Dominican Republic with Dominica and Guinea-Bissau with Guinea.

ROPHALIC referring to a cumulative song, poem or sentence which adds something to every verse or word. E.g. the rhyme, 'There was an old lady who swallowed a fly'. Or this sentence where each successive word is longer by one letter, 'I do not like these shoddy idiotic rophalic sentences.'

ROOSEVELT the name of two US Presidents, Teddy
Roosevelt, the 26th President, and his distant cousin
Franklin Delano Roosevelt (FDR) the 32nd. FDR was the
only President to win four Presidential elections. His
opponents pointed out the ROOSEVELT is an anagram of
VOTE LOSER but unfortunately for them this was quite
inappropriate.

ROTUNDA should really mean a pseudonym. E.g.
Charles Dodgson ROTUNDA the name of Lewis Carroll.

RUBBERNECK an over-inquisitive or gaping person who
twists around to see things. Rubberneck is also
something you can do to relax your wife.

RUBENESQUE describing a plump or voluptuous woman.
It is derived from the Flemish painter Sir Peter Paul
Rubens (1577-1640) whose paintings often featured this
body type.

RUPTUREWORT a plant that has long been used to make
medicines. It was once thought to cure hernia (hence the
name). Rupturewort is also the longest word you can
form using only the top row letters on the keyboard.

RUN For a long time SET was SET at the top as the word with the most different meanings at about 430. But after a strong RUN, RUN is now recognised as the champion with some 640 meanings.

S

SABOTAGE deliberate damage to machinery. E.g. clogging up the works by placing a shoe in a machine to prevent it from working. *Sabot* is the French word for a wooden shoe. Sabotage was used by the French Resistance in World War Two.

SADISM and MASOCHISM are EPONYMS. They are named after two notorious aristocratic writers Frenchman Donatien Francois, the Marquis de Sade and Austrian Leopold von Sacher-Masoch.

SAFARI is the Swahili word for journey.

SAHARA rather disappointingly, Sahara means just desert in Arabic.

SALARY comes from the Latin *salarium,* the sum given to Roman soldiers to buy salt, from *sal* salt.

SALLY a strange alteration of the girl's name Sarah. Other such strange alterations are Del for Derek, Hal for Harry, Moll for Mary, and Tel for Terence.

SALMONELLA micro-organisms responsible for food-poisoning and other serious illnesses such as typhoid. Nothing to do with the fish salmon but called after Doctor D.E. Salmon (1850--1914), an American pathologist. Also unrelated to that mythical couple Sam 'n Ella.

SALVER in ancient times kings were paranoid about being poisoned. A servant was employed to taste the king's food to see if it was safe. The tested food was presented on a salver, from the Latin *salvare*, to save, from which we also get SALVATION.

SAMOVAR a Russian tea urn. In Russian the word samovar means self-boil.

A samovar

SANCTION has two opposite meanings. It means to allow, but it also means to forbid.

SANDWICH refers to John Montagu (1718-1792), Fourth Earl of Sandwich, an inveterate gambler who ate slices of cold meat between bread at the gaming table during marathon sessions rather than get up for a proper meal.

SANDWICH BOARD a former advertising medium whereby a man walked around sandwiched between two boards carrying marketing messages.

SANSKRIT the ancient literary language of India. From the Sanskrit *samskrta,* put together.

SARCOPHAGUS a stone coffin. Originally a type of stone used for coffins which the Greeks believed would consume the flesh of corpses. Sarcophagus literally means flesh eating in Greek.

SARDINE there is really no such fish as a sardine. What are called sardines are usually young pilchards.

SARDONIC bitter or mockingly scornful. From the Greek *sardonios,* a plant from Sardinia which was so bitter that it screwed up the face of the eater.

SASSENACH the Gaelic Scottish name for an English person, with its origins in Saxony, Germany. It gives rise to the Gaelic word for BREXIT, which is SASSAMACH, from *amach,* out.

SATAN nobody seems to have a good to say about this poor old devil. But before his fall, his angelic name was Lucifer, which means bearer of light.

SATURNINE dark and gloomy like the planet Saturn. Other adjectives which reflect the supposed properties of planets are mercurial from Mercury and jovial from Jupiter.

SAWNEY an English nickname for a Scotsman. It may be a corruption of 'Sandy'. The English also use Jock for the same purpose.

SAXOPHONE a woodwind instrument made of brass invented by the Belgian, Adolphe Sax, in the 1840s. There is very little classical music written for the saxophone because great composers like Mozart, Bach or Beethoven never heard one. Saxophone is probably the only word containing the sequence xop.

SAUNA is the only Finnish word in common use in English.

SCAPEGOAT someone who takes the blame for the failings or misdeeds of others. Once a year the Jewish high priest would send a goat into the wilderness on the Day of Atonement as a symbolic bearer of the sins of the people.

SCHADENFREUDE a malicious pleasure in the misfortunes of others. A German word from *Schade* hurt and *Freude* joy.

SCHLEP to move slowly or drag. From the Yiddish *schlepen*, to drag.

SCHMALTZ excessive sentimentality. From the Yiddish *shmalts*, meaning melted fat.

SCHMOOZE to chat persuasively so as to gain favour. From the Yiddish *shmuesn,* to chat.

SCHOOL comes from a Greek word *schole* meaning leisure.

SCHOOLMASTER is an anagram of THE CLASSROOM.

SCIAPODOUS having very large feet. From the name the Greeks used for the legendary inhabitants of the hot deserts of Africa. Pliny wrote that these people lay on their backs, during extreme heat, and protected themselves from the sun by the shade of their feet.

SCISSORS is a plural word for which there is no singular. Other such words include eaves, alms and pliers.

SCRABBLE this was not the first name of this famous game. It was originally called Lexico and then Criss Cross before finally being called Scrabble.

SCREENAGER a young person who spends a lot of time on the internet and computers.

SCROOTCHED means crouched or hunched up. At 10 letters it is the nearly the longest word of just one syllable but overtaken by SQUIRRELLED.

SCRUMPTIOUS delicious, delightful. Probably a corruption of sumptuous. Roald Dahl inserted diddly to make the word scrumdiddlyumptious, used by Willy Wonka in the novel, Charlie and the Chocolate Factory.

SCUBA is an acronym for Self-Contained Underwater Breathing Apparatus.

SCURRYFUNGE a very rapid tidying of your house when unexpected visitors are seen at the gate.

SCUTTLEBUTT the cask on a ship containing drinking water. It was a small barrel, a butt, which had been scuttled or holed so that the water could be retrieved. Sailors would often gather around the scuttlebutt to chat, so the word has taken on the meaning of rumour or gossip.

SECRETARY a clerical assistant but originally a person entrusted with secrets. No change there!

SELFISH what they do at the seafood store.

SELFIE a picture of oneself usually taken on a mobile phone and displayed on social media. SHELFIE is a selfie with a bookshelf in the background to give the impression of intelligence and erudition.

SEMINAR and SEMEN both come from the same Latin root, *semen*, meaning seed.

SENSELESSNESS (or possibly SENSELESSNESSES) is the longest word using one vowel several times.

SEQUOIA the giant redwood tree, is a six letter common word containing all five vowels. But also see IOUEA.

SERENDIPITY a happy and unexpected discovery or a fortunate accident. The English politician and historian Horace Walpole coined the word in 1754 from the title of the fairy tale, The Three Princes of Serendip, a story in which the heroes 'were always making discoveries, by accidents and sagacity, of things they were not in quest of'. Serendip was a former name for Sri Lanka.

SERPENTINE snakelike, winding, tortuous. For Londoners the Serpentine is a curved lake in Hyde Park.

SESQUIPEDALIAN having many syllables; another word for POLYSYLLABIC. Originally used to deride pretentious writers who used long obscure words. It literally means a foot and a half long, from the Latin *sesqui,* one and half and *pes,* foot.

SEXAGENARIAN a person aged between sixty and seventy. But the word is sometimes misunderstood as in, 'A sexagenarian at his age - I think that's disgusting'.

SHAMPOO derived from the Hindustani word *champo,* meaning rub.

SHRAPNEL Fragments of any shell or bomb scattered by an explosion. The word sounds German, but this lethal device was invented by the British General H. Shrapnel (1761-1842) during the Peninsular War.

SHACONIAN someone who believes that Francis Bacon wrote Shakespeare's plays.

SHAKALSHAS were a people emigrating from Phrygia and colonizing Sicily in early times. It is the longest word which can be typed using only the middle row of letters on the keyboard.

SHAMBLES we have all experienced a shambles meaning a mess or a muddle, but did you know that a shambles was originally an animal slaughterhouse?

SHAMROCK the emblem of Ireland is the harp, not the shamrock. And Ireland's official colour is blue, not green.

SHERMAN sherman tanks are called after American General William Sherman. He had the very unusual middle name of Tecumseh.

SHERRY A fortified wine, which takes its name from Jerez, a town in Spain. Port takes its name from Oporto in Portugal.

SHIBBOLETH a test word or phrase which will betray an infiltrator from a hostile tribe. From the Old Testament where the Ephraimites were exposed by their incorrect pronunciation of the word shibboleth (which means ear of corn in Hebrew).

SHITTIM the wood of the SHITTAH tree, a species of acacia mentioned in the Old Testament.

SHYSTER an unscrupulous and dishonest professional, especially in the areas of law or politics. Believed to be derived from the German, *scheisser*, a defecator.

SHLIMAZL someone who is always unlucky. A Yiddish word.

SHOPLIFTER An anagram of A SHOPLIFTER is HAS TO PILFER.

SHREW a small mouselike animal. It was wrongly believed to be venomous for cattle. Hence it came to mean evil or troublesome. Shrewish often refers to a scolding woman. But from the same etymon, Shrewd came to mean crafty or clever.

SIDEBURNS strips whiskers or hair at the sides of the face. The word began as burnsides and was named after U.S. Army General Ambrose Burnside (1824-81) who sported them. Over time the word's two syllables swapped places.

SILHOUETTE a shadow picture of a person in profile showing outline only and filled in with black. Called after Etienne de Silhouette, a French politician. In 1759 he made petty economies and being too mean to have a proper portrait of himself painted, had a silhouette done instead.

SIMILE something like a metaphor.

SINECURE a well-paid job that requires very little work. From the Latin *sine cura*, without care.

SINGAPORE means Lion City. From the Malay *Singa*, lion and *Pura*, city.

SIRIUS is the brightest star in the night sky. It is called the dog star because it is in the constellation Canis Major (the great dog). Sirius is approaching our solar system at 5 km per second, so one day we could be in Sirius trouble.

SISYPHEAN ineffective, endless and useless. In Greek mythology Sisyphus was a king who annoyed the gods. He was consequently condemned for eternity to roll a huge rock up a long, steep hill only to see it roll back down.

SKEDADDLE to scram or run away. American Civil War military slang of unknown origin.

SLOGAN originally a Celtic war cry. From the Gaelic *sluagh* army and *gairm* cry.

SLUBBERDEGULLION a dirty and nasty little fellow. Probably from the Dutch *slubberen*, slurping.

SMILES the longest word in the language because there is a mile between the first and last letter.

SMOKING if smoking is so bad for you how come it cures kippers?

SNARK an imaginary animal invented by Lewis Carroll in his poem, The Hunting of the Snark, in 1876.

SNICKERSNEE a long dangerous knife used in fighting. From the Dutch *steken* to thrust and *snijden* to cut.

SNOLLYGOSTER a clever, unscrupulous person, a politician who cares more for personal gain than serving the people. An American word derived from Pennsylvania German *schnelle geeschter*, from German *schnell* quick and *Geist* spirit.

SNOWFLAKE a disparaging term for someone who is overly sensitive.

SOCK. 'Put a sock in it' means reduce the volume of noise. From the days when a huge phonograph could be muted by literally putting a sock in it.

SOLEMN has two anagrams, both fruit - LEMONS and MELONS.

SOLIDUS the oblique stroke (/) used between words, as in man/woman, or in fractions such as 3/4. Also called a slash, diagonal, separatrix, virgule, shilling, or slant.

SOLSTICE the time when the sun reaches its maximum distance from the equator. In the northern hemisphere the summer solstice is usually on June 21 and the winter solstice on December 21. From the Latin *sol*, sun, *sistere*, to stand still.

SOON was the Anglo-Saxon word for now.

SPAM meaning junk mail originally came from a Monty Python sketch about tinned meat.

SPARKLEMUFFIN a brightly coloured species of peacock spider found in Australia. It can jump fifty times its own length.

SPECTRUM is an anagram of CRUMPETS.

SPHENO PALATINE GANGLEONEURALGIA is the technical term for an ice cream headache.

SPIC a derogatory term for a Spanish-speaking person from Central or South America. Probably a contraction of 'no speak English'.

SOPHOMORE A second year student. This is a rare example of a single word OXYMORON from the Greek *sophos*, wise and *moros*, foolish. Presumably because such students had to be able to argue both sides of an issue.

SPINSTER an unmarried woman often of advancing years. In past times, one of the few employments open to such people was spinning wool and hence the word.

SPLIT INFINITIVE it is ungrammatical to ever split an infinitive.

SPOONERISM a deliberate or accidental transposition of initial letters or sounds of spoken words. E.g. town drain instead of down train. Named after the Revered William Spooner (1844-1930) an Oxford don and leading exponent of this form of speech.

SPOONFEED is the longest word with all its letters in reverse alphabetical order. WRONGED is the right answer if you do not allow double letters. See AEGILOPS.

SOUPSPOONS the longest word we can find in which all the letters come from the second half of the alphabet.

SPRING TIDE This has nothing to do with the season of Spring but comes from to spring forth. Spring tides occur twice a month all the year round when the sun and the moon are in alignment, making high tides higher and low tides lower. When the sun and the moon are at right angles to the earth, we get a NEAP tide, a word that comes from Middle English, meaning small.

SPUD this name for a potato comes from the fact that a spud was a narrow flat spade used to dig potatoes.

SPUTNIK the first artificial satellite to be launched into space in 1957. The word means travelling companion in Russian.

SQUASH a sport, more properly called squash racquets, which gets its name from the fact that the little ball used can be squashed in the hand.

SQUIRRELLED at 11 letters the longest word pronounced as one syllable.

STALACTITE an icicle-like formation of calcium carbonate which hangs from the roof of a cave, formed by slow deposition from dripping water. It is in contrast with a STALAGMITE which forms upwards on the floor of the cave by the same process. And how does one remember which is which? Well, tights go down!

STARBOARD the right-hand side of the ship when pointing forward. From the old English *steorbord*, literally steer-board. Vikings steered their ships with a board on the right-hand side of the boat.

STARBUCKS the famous coffee house takes its name from Starbuck, Captain Ahab's first mate in the book Moby Dick by Herman Melville.

STARTLING is the longest word which makes a new word every time a letter is removed (starting, staring, string, sting, sing, sin, in, I).

STATIONARY and STATIONERY are often confused. Stationary (containing A for automobile) means not moving, while stationery (containing E for envelope) refers to paper and office supplies.

STAYCATION a stay at home vacation. A PORTMANTEAU word.

STEEPLECHASE a horse race run over fields, hedges and walls. The first official such race was run over four miles from the steeple of St. John's Church in Buttevant County Cork in Ireland to the steeple of St. Mary's Church in Doneraile. The race was organised as a result of a wager between two local men, O'Callaghan and Blake. The most famous modern steeplechase is the Grand National, run annually at Aintree near Liverpool.

STENCH a bad smell or odour. From the Saxon *stanc* which became STINK. Stench is to stink as drench is to drink.

STET an instruction to a printer to disregard a correction and let the original remain. From the Latin *stet*, let it stand.

STEWARD originally a keeper of pigs, it came to mean anybody in charge of anything. From the Old English *stigweard*, based on *stig*, a pen for pigs or cattle, and *weard*, a guardian or keeper.

STIGMA a mark of shame or discredit, a stain. From the Greek *stizein*, to tattoo. Stigmata are bodily marks or pains resembling the wounds of the crucified Jesus. The first person said to have experienced stigmata is St. Francis of Assisi, in the 13th century.

STREAKING is an anagram of GREAT SKIN.

STIFLE is the only word which is an anagram of ITSELF.

STOCHASTIC something that depends on a random distribution of probabilities. From the Greek *stokhastikos* able to guess, conjecturing.

STOIC someone indifferent to pleasure or pain and who never complains. Originally a member of a school of philosophy founded by Zeno of Citium about 300 B.C. holding that the wise man should be free from passion and unmoved by joy or grief. From the Greek *stoa*, a porch referring to the hall where Zeno taught.

STRABISMUS a technical word for a squint in the eye. The name was made famous by the humorist J.B. Morton (Beachcomber) in the Daily Express who introduced a character called Dr Strabismus of Utrecht (whom God preserve).

STRAFE a famous German propaganda slogan in World War I was "Gott Strafe England!" or "God punish England." British troops adopted the word strafe to mean a heavy bombardment or fire or even a sharp reprimand.

STRAWBERRY a strawberry is not actually a true berry, because its seeds or achenes are not enclosed by juicy pulp, as are those of a raspberry or a blackberry. A strawberry is technically an aggregate accessory fruit.

STRENGTHS is the longest word with just one vowel used once.

STRONTIUM a light metallic chemical element. It is named after Strontian, a parish in Argyllshire, Scotland, the site of lead mines where Strontium was first discovered.

STROGANOFF Beef Stroganoff is beef with sour-cream sauce over noodles. Named after Count Paul Stroganoff, a 19th century Russian diplomat.

STROKE meaning a medical condition affecting the heart is a shortened version of the expression 'A Stroke of God's hand.'

STRYCHNINE starts with seven consonants and ends with nine.

STYMIE to prevent another person from achieving a desired goal. Used in croquet and initially in golf to prevent an opponent from holing out. In the game of snooker, you can stymie your opponent by laying a snooker from which the name of the game is derived.

SUBBOOKKEEPER the only word which contains four successive pairs of double letters.

SUBCONTINENTAL has all five vowels in reverse alphabetical order.

SUBTERFUGE a deceptive device or stratagem. From the Latin *subter*, meaning underneath and *fugere*, to flee. So a scheme to fly under the RADAR.

SUCURUJUS is the longest word containing only the vowel U and the longest word with U as every alternating letter. A Sucuruju is a South American anaconda.

SULTANA a dried grape much used in baking cakes etc. It is called after the wife of a Sultan.

SUNBURN Only two mammals suffer from sunburn - humans and pigs.

SUPERCALIFRAGILISTICEXPIALIDOCIOUS is the title of a song from the 1964 Disney musical, Mary Poppins. The first example of its use dates to 1931. Its meaning at the time was given as something that was 'grand, great, glorious, splendid, superb, wonderful'. Inverness Caledonian Thistle secured a shock 3-1 Scottish Cup win over the mighty Celtic football club in February 2000. This led to a famous headline in the Sun newspaper – Super Cally go Ballistic, Celtic are atrocious.

SUPERCILIOUS patronising, haughty or contemptuous. From the Latin where it literally means eyebrow, referring to the raising the eyebrow to express haughtiness.

SUPERFLUOUS unnecessary, redundant. From Latin *superfluous*, literally overflowing, from *super* over and *fluere* to flow (from which we get fluent).

SUPEREGO a term coined by Sigmund Freud. The superego is the ethical component of the personality and provides the moral standards by which the ego operates. It might be what Superman thinks of himself.

SUPERGRASS a renegade who informs on or betrays many people, perhaps former friends or allies. The origin of the term grass signifying an informer comes from the expression 'snake in the grass', which has a similar meaning.

SUPPEDANEUM a support for the feet of somebody being crucified.

SURD an irrational real number such as the square root of 2 which cannot be expressed as the ratio of two integers a/b. It comes from the Latin *surdus* meaning deaf and is related to the word absurd.

SWAT as in SWAT TEAM is an acronym for Special Weapons and Tactics.

SWEETBREAD a menu description of the pancreas of a cow or sheep. Used so as not to upset diners.

SWIMS is the longest word which looks the same upside down. NOON, NON and MOW do the same.

SYNECDOCHE a figure of speech in which a part is used to refer to the whole or vice versa. E,g, 'Here comes the army' when a single officer enters; or the British Tommy referring to the whole British Army. From the Greek *syn* together and *ekdechesthai* to receive.

SYLLOGISM A Greek concept of logic involving three statements. E.g. All Spartans are Greek, Dimis is Spartan, therefore Dimis is Greek. A SILLYGISM is a parody of a syllogism e.g. The more you learn, the more you forget; the more you forget, the less you know; therefore, the more you learn, the less you know.

SYNONYM a word having the same meaning.
Something to use when you cannot spell the original word you wanted to use. From the Greek *syn*, with and *onoma*, word.

SYZYGY an alignment of three celestial bodies.
Pronounced SIZ-I-JEE. A six-letter word with no vowels,
two Ys and a Z. A heavy scorer at Scrabble.

TABOO forbidden or excluded. From the Polynesian language of the island of Tonga *ta-bu,* sacred. First mentioned in Captain Cook's book 'A Voyage to the Pacific Ocean' in 1793.

TANDEM a bicycle made for two. The person in front is called the 'captain' who steers the vehicle. The person behind is called the 'stoker' who supplies the main power. The captain also informs the unsighted stoker what the traffic is doing. The name is a pun on the Latin word *tandem* which means 'at length'.

TANGELO a rare citrus fruit, a cross between a TANGERINE and a pomelo or grapefruit. Another portmanteau word.

TANGERINE is an anagram of ARGENTINE. The only English football team which plays in a tangerine strip is Blackpool F.C.

TAPPEN a rectal plug used by a bear during hibernation. It is usually composed of pine leaves and hardened feces. The tappen is expelled by the bear upon waking in spring. Disgusting for us but quite natural for the bear.

TARAMASALATAS the longest word involving consonants alternating with the same one vowel.

TATTERDEMALIAN a ragged and wretched fellow. A ragamuffin.

TAUROMACHY a polite name for bull-fighting. From the Greek *tauros*, a bull, and *makhe*, fighting.

TAUTOLOGY repeating yourself twice.

TAWDRY cheap, showy, or poor quality – particularly of clothing. A corruption of Saint Audrey, an English nun from the 7th century. Rich people looked down on St Audrey's lace which was sold at St Audrey's fair in Ely in England.

TAXI is the English word which is most understood around the world by non-English speakers (though the abbreviation OK is also widely known). Each letter has vertical symmetry. Taxi is spelled this way in most languages. However, in Irish Gaelic, it is spelled Tacsai because there is no X in the Irish alphabet.

TELEVISION is a word disliked by LOGOPHILES because it mixes two sources. It comes from *tele*, the Greek for far, and *videre* the Latin to see. Incidentally television is called a medium because it never contains anything rare or well done.

TENNIS The modern game was originally called sphairistike, meaning 'pertaining to a ball or a sphere'. This was shortened to sticky, but such a clumsy term soon vanished. The name tennis comes from the French *tenez* hold or receive.

TERGIVERSATION turning your back on a cause or belief. From the Latin *tergo*, back and *vertere* to turn.

TERRIER a hunting dog renowned for its ability to dig burrowing animals out of the earth. From the Latin *terra* meaning earth.

TESTICLE comes from the Latin *testis* meaning witness, which is also the source of testify, testament and testimony. A testicle was evidence (or witness) of virility. It is believed that this might be derived from the ancient practice of men hold their testicles when swearing an oath.

TEXT and TEXTILE come from the same root, the Latin *textus* woven. A thought is a thread, and a story is woven from thoughts.

THALER an old German silver coin from which we get the word dollar.

A thaler

THE is the most commonly used word in the English language. (Thrice in that sentence!)

THESAURUS is literally a treasure chest – from the Greek *thesauros*. Some children think that a thesaurus is a kind of dinosaur which has become extinct, dead, obsolete, extinguished or no longer existing.

THEREIN is a seven-letter word which contains 12 separate words without any rearrangement – therein, the, there, he, her, here, herein, ere, re, rein, in I.

THEY is the plural form of HE, SHE and IT. No other plural has three distinct singular forms (unless you count THEIR).

THISLETWEEKER a lovely old name for a goldfinch.

THUG comes from the Hindi word *thag,* referring to fanatical followers of the goddess Kali. They roamed India killing and robbing people.

TIGON a cross between a male tiger and a female lion. A pairing of a male lion with a female tiger is called a liger.

TILDE the sign ~ placed over the letter 'n' in Spanish to indicate a palatalized sound.

TIMBROLOGY an alternative name for philately or stamp collecting.

TIN is a silvery metal. With the symbol Sn (from Latin: *stannum*) and atomic number 50, Tin is the element with the shortest name – just three letters. A tin can contains very little tin; it is over 90% steel.

TINSEL comes from the Latin *scintilla*, a spark.

TIN PAN ALLEY a term for the New York centre for composers and publishers of popular music. A tin pan was a name for a tuneless old piano.

TIRAMISU the dessert means 'pick me up' or 'cheer me up' in Italian.

TITFER a hat. Cockney rhyming slang based on tit for tat.

TITTLE the dot on an i is a tittle.

TO,TOO, TWO Three common words with the same sound but different meanings. They can be used consecutively in a meaningful sentence: I donate to two charities, and my wife donates to two too.

TOAST to toast a person arose from the custom of dropping a piece of toasted bread into a glass of wine to improve its flavour. The charcoal in burnt toast absorbs the acid in wine.

TOBAGO is an island in the Caribbean. It is named after the Spanish for tobacco *tabaco* because the island is shaped like a fat cigar. TOBAGO is an anagram of BOGOTA, the capital of Colombia.

TOKYO the capital of Japan is an anagram for KYOTO, a former capital of Japan.

TOMBOLA a kind of lottery or raffle often involving a rotating container from which tickets are drawn. From the Italian, *tombolare*, to tumble or perform a cartwheel.

TONTINE a scheme whereby people pool their money and the last surviving person gets it all. Named after the Italian banker Lorenzo Tonti (1635-1690) who first devised the scheme.

TOOTHSOME an old word meaning something tasty or desirable.

TOOT-TOOT is a palindromic word which looks exactly the same as its mirror image.

TOOT SWEET quickly, immediately. This is a corruption of the French 'tout de suite', which means all at once.

TOMATO comes from the Aztec Nahuatl *tomatl.* When first introduced to Europe the tomato was grown as an ornamental plant and the fruit was not eaten. TOMATO is a word with vertical symmetry.

TORY another name for a British Conservative politician, but derived from the Gaelic word *toraidh* meaning outlaw or highwayman.

A TOYOTA is a car which looks the same whether coming or going. So is a RACECAR.

TRAGEDY comes from the Greek *tragodia* which literally means goat songs. Apparently Athenian actors in ancient times wore goat skins when performing on stage.

TRAILERS movie trailers got their name because they were originally shown after the movie.

TRISKAIDEKAPHOBIA a morbid fear of the number thirteen. Believed by many to stem from the fact that there were thirteen people at table at the Last Supper. Thirteen's place as the unluckiest of the primes, was recently challenged by nineteen, because of Covid 19.

TRIVIA is the plural of the Latin word *trivium*, a place where three roads meet. Hence a public place and common or commonplace. In classical times trivium also means studies which consisted of grammar, rhetoric, and logic, forming the lower division of the quadrivium of the seven liberal arts. Trivia is one of those words which is rarely heard in the singular. Others include scampi, measles and assizes.

TROGLODYTE a cave-dweller. A person who is primitive or has outdated attitudes. From the Greek *trogle*, a cave.

TROIKA a Russian word meaning a vehicle drawn by three horses. It is used to refer to a team of three people or a triumvirate.

TROLLIED meaning DRUNK has all its letters in reverse alphabetical order.

TROUSAL a cross between a trout and a salmon bred in the West of Ireland.

TROUSERS comes from the Gaelic *triubhas* or Irish *trius*. The singular of trousers was originally trews.

TRUCULENT a vehicle that someone borrowed.

TRUMPERY means showy and worthless stuff, complete nonsense. We should have known! From the French *tromper* to deceive.

TULIP a flower often associated with the Netherlands but which originated in Turkey. The word tulip comes from the Turkish word for turban, *tulbent*. So called from the resemblance of the flower to a turban.

TUNGSTEN is a chemical element with atomic number 74. It is used in light bulb filaments. It has the highest melting point, 3,422 °C, and highest boiling point, 5,930 °C, of any element. It is much denser than lead. The name is Swedish and means heavy stone. Its symbol is W for Wolframium which it was sometimes called.

TURKEY originally a name for a guinea fowl imported through Turkish territory. The modern American turkey was so called because of its resemblance to the guinea fowl.

TWELVE in old English *twelf* comes from the old Germanic *twalif*, a compound of *twa* two and *lif* left over i.e. two left over after having already counted to ten. It is remarkable that TWELVE PLUS ONE is an anagram of ELEVEN PLUS TWO.

TWENTY-NINE is spelled with letters made up of straight lines only. Twenty-nine of them to be precise. It is the only number whose name has this property.

TWICHILD a person in his or her second childhood.

TWIDDLE To turn about with the fingers, especially a radio dial. A combination of twirl and fiddle.

TWINS wombmates.

TYPEWRITER all the letters of the word are found on the top line of the typewriter keyboard.

UCALEGON a neighbour whose house is on fire or has burnt down. Someone who is in big trouble. Ucalegon, as mentioned in the Aeneid, was one of the Elders of Troy, whose house was set afire by the Achaeans when they sacked the city.

UGLI A fruit made by crossing an orange, a grapefruit and a TANGERINE. It really is a very ugly looking fruit.

UGSOME loathsome or frightful. From Old Norse *ugga,* to fear.

U.K. The country with the longest name in the world is The United Kingdom of Great Britain and Northern Ireland.

UKULELE a four-stringed musical instrument. The word is Hawaiian and means a jumping flea. From *uku,* flea and *lele* jumping.

ULLAGE a word for the empty space between the top of a bottle and the liquid.

218

ULTRACREPIDATE to criticise beyond the sphere of one's knowledge. From an old Roman story about the painter, Apelles. A cobbler criticised the sandals in one his paintings. When the cobbler went on to criticise other parts of the painting Apelles said, *ne sutor ultra crepidum,* the cobbler must not go beyond the sandal.

ULULATE to utter a long, loud, high-pitched noise especially as an expression of sorrow. From the Latin *ululare,* to howl or shriek.

UMBELLIFEROUS A family of herbaceous plants typically having hollow stems, and flowers in umbels: it includes fennel, dill, parsley, carrot, celery, and parsnip.

UMBLES the entrails of an animal – particularly a deer. Umble pie was made from the heart, liver etc of a deer. To eat humble pie is to humble oneself or eat one's words.

UMPIRE from the Latin *non par* – someone who is not on par with the others. In French it became *noumpere,* which was heard as an umpire.

UNCOMPLIMENTARY and UNSPORTSMANLIKE are two fifteen letter words which contain all the vowels. They are believed to be the longest such words.

UNCOPYRIGHTABLE is the longest English word with no repeated letters.

UNDEFINABILITY is an anagram of UNIDENTIFIABLY

UNDERGROUND an 11 letter word which begins and ends with UND.

UNDERSTUDY has four consecutive letters in alphabetical order – RSTU.

UNDERTAKER somebody who always lets his customers down.

UNIQUE You are unique; just like everyone else. A nice little PARADOX to ponder.

UNPROSPEROUSNESSES meaning states of lacking prosperity, is the longest word in which no letter appears just once.

URCHIN a mischievous child, especially a boy in ragged clothes. It comes from the old French *herichon* and the Latin *ericisius* – a hedgehog. An urchin from London might tell you that urchin was under 'er mouth.

USA a little Japanese town changed its name to USA so it could label all of its industrial export production as MADE IN USA.

USHER an usher is an old word for an assistant teacher. Perhaps they had to 'ush the children. The word usher contains four personal pronouns – us, she, he and her.

UZZARD is an archaic word meaning the letter Z. It also meant a second-generation illegitimate person, the bastard son of a bastard son.

UZI a type of submachine gun that is named after its designer Israeli Major Uziel Gal.

An Uzi

VACCINE comes from the Latin *vacca*, cow. English country doctor Edward Jenner (1749-1823) used cowpox material in his research which led to an effective vaccine against smallpox. Some estimate that his work saved more lives than that of any other person.

VAGINA is the Latin word for scabbard.

VANILLA the flavour of the vanilla bean which is from a type of orchid. Vanilla has come to mean plain or conventional because vanilla ice cream was considered the standard. Originally vanilla was regarded as an aphrodisiac because its pod resembled a vagina. Vanilla comes from the Spanish for 'little vagina'.

VALETUDINARIAN a sickly person who is always worried about their health. From the Latin *valetudinarius*, meaning state of health (good or bad).

VAMP a woman who uses her charms to seduce or exploit. An abbreviation of vampire.

VENEZUELA means Little Venice in Spanish. Supposedly the name was given by Americo Vespucci in 1499 when he saw a native village built on stilts above the water in a lake.

VENTRILOQUIST from the Latin *venter* stomach and *loqui* to speak. Based on the mistaken belief that ventriloquists operated by forcing air through their stomachs.

VENUS is the only planet that rotates clockwise. It is named after the Roman goddess of love.

VERBICIDE the 'killing' of a word by perversion from its original meaning. E.G. the word 'literally' has been subject to verbicide. People use it in literally every sentence to literally mean something different from what it literally means.

VERISIMILITUDES is the longest word alternating consonants and vowels. A verisimilitude is something that appears to be true. From the Latin *verus* true and *similis* like.

VERNIER an instrument for making tiny delicate measurements. It is named after the French mathematician, Pierre Vernier (1580--1637), who invented it.

VERSO and RECTO are the names for the left-hand page and the right-hand page of a book, respectively.

VEXILLOLOGIST a person who studies flags. Perhaps they get angry or unwell if you damage a flag.

VIGESIMAL relating to a system where one counts in twenties rather than tens, which is the decimal system. The Babylonians used the sexagesimal system, counting in sixties, and some remnants of this remain even today - sixty minutes in an hour, for example.

VERB comes from the Latin, *verbum*, meaning a word. A verb is said to be weak if its past tense is derived from the present by the addition of '-ed'. For example, 'walk' becomes 'walked'. On the other hand, a verb is said to be strong, if the past tense is formed by an internal vowel change. For example, 'give' becomes 'gave'. Curiously, some UK weak verbs become strong verbs in the US. For example, 'dive' becomes 'dived' in the UK, but 'dove' in the US.

VERBIFY to make into a verb. This is frowned on when seen today but has been common for hundreds of years. Words which started as nouns and are now used as verbs include bed, sleep, fool, stop, drink and talk.

VIATICUM an allowance such as food or money for a journey. It is also the term for the Christian Eucharist given to a dying person – as a provision for their final journey.

VILLAIN originally meant a serf, or a peasant attached to a farm or villa. But because of poverty and poor living conditions, such people often turned to crime and of course the meanings of such words were determined by the educated upper classes.

VINDEMY the stealing of honey from beehives. It is not illegal unless the hives belong to someone else, but the bees certainly do not approve of it. From the Latin *vindemiatus* – to gather the vintage.

VINEGAR literally sick wine from the Latin *vinum*, wine, and *aegrum*, sick.

VIRAGO originally a heroic woman or a female warrior, literally a woman who was man-like from the Latin *vir*, man. The word came to mean a domineering or bad-tempered woman.

VIRTUALLY comes from the same root as virtue and originally meant 'showing the virtues of' so a brave man was virtually a lion. Meanwhile, virtue meant manly as it comes from the Latin *vir,* man, from whence we get virility.

VITAMIN is from the Polish word *vitamine* coined by biochemist Kazimierz Funk in 1912. There are 13 vitamins—vitamins A, C, D, E, K, and the B vitamins (thiamine, riboflavin, niacin, pantothenic acid, biotin, B6, B12, and folate).

VIZ an abbreviation for the Latin word *videlicet* which means 'that is to say'.

VLOG a BLOG with video content. First used in 2002. A word with the rare beginning of vl.

VODKA means little water in Russian and Polish.

VOMITORY maybe not what you think! In a Roman amphitheatre it is a passage by which the crowd is let out. From the same Latin root as vomit.

VOLT, AMP, OHM are electrical units which are EPONYMS. The volt is the unit of electromotive force, named after the Italian Alessandro Volta (1745-1827). The amp is the unit of electric current, named after French scientist Andre Marie Ampere (1775-1836), and the ohm is the unit of electric resistance, named after Georg Ohm (1787-1854).

WALLABY someone who aspires to be a kangaroo.

WALLA-WALLA a film scene in which people in a crowd pretend to be talking to each other but are merely saying 'walla-walla' all the time. The theatrical equivalent is 'rhubarb, rhubarb'.

WARLOCK originally a liar on oath or a traitor. From the Old Norse *varar,* a solemn promise or vow. Nowadays, merely an evil wizard.

WASSAIL a greeting to a guest when presenting a drink. From the Old Norse, *ves heill*, be in good health.

WEDNESDAY is Woden's day, after Woden the Norse god of victory. Other days of the week are derived from Viking gods. Friday is named after Frigg, the goddess of love, Tuesday after Tiw, the god of war, and Thursday after Thor, the god of thunder.

WETWARE a computer programmer's term for the human brain which is 80% water. As distinct from hardware and software.

WHATCHAMACALLIT another word for a thingamajig or even a doohickie. Something whose name you cannot remember.

WHIFF-WHAFF the forerunner of ping pong or table tennis. According to Boris Johnson, it was invented in England and played on dining room tables.

WHIPPERSNAPPER a cheeky or impudent lad, a young person considered to be presumptuous or overconfident.

WHISKY (or WHISKEY in Ireland and the USA) is from the Gaelic *uisge beatha* meaning water of life. Similarly, the French call brandy *eau de vie* and the Swedes have a spirit called *aquavit*.

WHOOPEE an American shout of joy to denote extreme happiness. There is also the whoopee cushion, an air-filled bag which emits hilariously rude noises when sat upon.

WICKED meaning evil or vicious comes from the old English *wicca*, a wizard. In modern slang wicked has come to mean its opposite, wonderful. It is a CONTRANYM.

WIDDERSHINS or WITHERSHINS is an old word meaning moving anti-clockwise or contrary to the course of the sun. Demons always approached widdershins, so the word came to be associated with evil and bad luck. The opposite of widdershins is DEASIL meaning a sunwise motion.

WIDOW is the only female word which is shorter than its corresponding male term WIDOWER.

WIKI a web page that can be quickly edited. From the Hawaiian *wikiwiki* very fast.

WILL a dead giveaway.

WILL-O'-THE-WISP a light that appears over marshy land at night, also known as jack-o-lantern or ignis fatuus. Some believed that it was of supernatural origin designed to lure followers to their doom, but scientists established that is due to the spontaneous combustion of gases such as methane or marsh gas. The term will-o'-

the-wisp is sometimes applied to an unreliable person who is difficult to pin down.

WINDBREAKER a protective garment or a primitive shelter for use at the beach; not someone who breaks wind all the time.

WINDOW a window was originally an unglazed hole in a roof. The word is from the Old Norse and literally means a wind eye; from *vindr* wind and *auga* eye. Some people think that WINDOW is what happens when you are successful at the lottery.

WINDSOR the British Royal Family was German in origin with the surname Saxe-Coburg-Gotha. After the outbreak of World War One, they dropped all contact with Germany and changed their surname to Windsor, after the name of Windsor Castle.

Windsor Castle

WINKLEPICKERS are shoes with such sharp points that they remind you of the tools used to prise winkles from their shells.

WYSIWYG a computer acronym for what you see is what you get.

WOEBEGONE beset with woe, sad or miserable in appearance.

WOKE actively attentive to issues of social and racial injustice. Past participle of wake. First used in this sense in 1972.

WOMYN an alternative spelling proposed by feminists who were worried that the word women contained the word men.

WOODBINE and HONEYSUCKLE two beautiful words for the same plant and flower.

WRENCH a female spanner.

X

XENODOCHEIONOLOGY is the study of hotels and inns. From the Greek *xenodocheion* inn.

XENOMANIA an inordinate attachment to foreign things. From the Greek *xenos*, guest or stranger.

XENOPHOBIA fear or hatred of foreigners and foreign things.

XHOSA the people and the language of a group of tribes from the Cape area in South Africa. The Xhosa language includes some unusual clicking sounds.

XEROX was registered 1952 as a trademark by Haloid Co. of Rochester, N.Y., for a copying device. Haloid became the XEROX Corporation in 1961. The word passed into common parlance as popular verb meaning to copy despite vigorous objections from the company's copyright department.

YAHOO a brutish savage from Swift's Gulliver's Travels. But nowadays an internet search engine.

YARBOROUGH a hand of thirteen cards containing no card higher than a nine. The Earl of Yarborough, who was a skilled mathematician, made money offering odds of a thousand to one against such a hand occurring. He had calculated that the true odds were closer to two thousand to one.

YCLEPT means 'called' as in 'Patrick, yclept Paddy'. Yclept is the past participle of an ancient word clepe (or cleep) meaning to call or name.

YE an old way of writing THE, but it is pronounced the same way as 'the'. In Hiberno-English, ye is still used as a plural for 'you' which has now vanished from standard English.

YEN an intense desire or longing. From Cantonese, *yan*, a craving or addiction (to opium).

YETI a Tibetan word. In Himalayan folklore a monstrous creature sometimes called the Abominable Snowman.

YLEM is the primordial matter of the universe in big bang theory.

YO-YO a toy consisting of a reel and length of string. From the Ilocano word *yoyo*. Ilocano is a language spoken in the Philippines. When something yo-yoes, it goes up and down e.g. the stock market.

YOU There are very few words ending in U. You is the commonest. Others include adieu, impromptu, menu, thou and PORTMANTEAU.

YTTERBY a small town in Sweden which is the only place in the world with four elements named after it. The chemical elements Yttrium, Terbium, Erbium, and Ytterbium were all discovered in minerals found in a local mine.

YULEHOLE the last available hole in a waist belt, often used after excessive food and drink at Christmas.

Z

ZA a slang term for pizza. Also the highest scoring two letter word in Scrabble. Place the Z on a triple letter square with the A across and down for a score of 62.

ZAFTIG having a pleasantly plump figure. From the Yiddish where it means juicy or succulent.

ZANY an unusual and extreme type of comedy. Originally a comic performer, a clown or buffoon. From the Italian Gianni, the name of a stock character in old comedies.

ZARF a holder for a coffee cup without a handle.

ZEBRA the word probably comes from Latin *equiferus,* wild horse. The stripe pattern on an individual zebra is as distinctive as human fingerprints.

ZED a word used by the British for the last letter of the English alphabet (Americans say zee). It was described by Shakespeare as 'Thou whoreson Z, thou unnecessary letter'.

ZEDLAND the English counties of Dorset, Somerset, and Devon, where Z replaces S in everyday speech.

ZELATRIX a nun whose job is to observe the behaviour of the sisters in her convent, including the postulants and the mother superior. From the same root as zealous.

ZENITH the point in the sky directly above the observer's head, the greatest height, the point at which something is at its most powerful or successful. From the Arabic *samt-ar-ras* direction of the head.

ZEUGMA a literary term for using one word to modify two other words in different ways. E.g., 'I lost my keys and my temper.' From the Greek *zeugma*, a yoking together.

ZIMBABWE means 'house of stones' in the Karanga dialect of Shona. The ancient Kingdom of Zimbabwe (c. 1000–1450) held the largest stone structures in precolonial Southern Africa.

ZIP as used in zip code; ZIP stands for 'zone improvement plan'.

ZODIAC an imaginary belt in the heavens. From the Greek word *zoion* meaning animals. Many of the signs of the zodiac are animals, e.g. Leo, Capricorn, Aries, Taurus, and Scorpio.

ZOMBIE is of West African origin and was originally the name of a snake god. Later it came to mean a reanimated corpse in voodoo cult.

ZONKEY a cross between a zebra and a donkey.

A zonkey

ZORRO a doglike fox found in South America.

ZYTHUM an ancient Egyptian beer. It was the last word in the dictionary until ZYZZYVA came along.

ZYZZYA a genus of tropical American weevils. The yellowish beetle was first discovered in 1922 in Brazil, and named by Thomas Lincoln Casey, Jr, an entomologist at New York's Museum of Natural History. It was probably named Zyzzyva as a practical joke to place it in a prominent ending position in guides and dictionaries.

Sources, References and Recommended Reading

The Chambers Dictionary

Merriam Webster US Dictionary

Etymonline.com

The Etymologicon by Mark Forsyth

World's Best Word Puzzles by Paul Sloane and Des MacHale

There are Tittles in This Title by Mitchell Symons

Oxford Dictionary of English Etymology by C.T. Onions

Word Nerd by Barbara Ann Kipfer.

The Uxbridge English Dictionary by Graeme Garden

Totally Weird and Wonderful Words by Erin McKean

The Authors

Paul Sloane was born in Johnstone, Scotland. He gained a first class degree in Engineering from Cambridge University. He came top of Sales School at IBM. He went on to become a Marketing Director, Managing Director and CEO of software companies. He and Des McHale have co-authored over 20 books of lateral thinking puzzles which have sold over 2 million copies in total. Paul's most popular business book is The Leader's Guide to Lateral Thinking Skills. He runs leadership master classes with top corporations around the world. He has been a visiting lecturer at Cambridge University, Lancaster University, Henley Business School and the Mumbai Institute of Technology. His Tedx talk is available on Youtube. It is entitled 'Are your Open-Minded?' He lives with his wife Ann, in Camberley England. They have three daughters and six grandchildren.

Desmond MacHale was born in Castlebar, Ireland. He holds B.Sc. and M.Sc. degrees in Mathematical Science from University College Galway and a Ph.D. in Algebra from the University of Keele in the UK. He is Emeritus Professor of Mathematics at University College Cork where he taught for forty years. He is the author of over sixty published books on such diverse topics as Lateral

Thinking Puzzles (with Paul Sloane), Wit, Jokes, Puzzles, Mathematical Humour, George Boole, John Ford's movie The Quiet Man, and Quitting Smoking. Among his interests are Geology, Photography, Music, Broadcasting, Words, Recreational Mathematics, Family History, and Puzzles of all kinds. He lives with his wife Anne in Cork and they have five children and three grandchildren.

Printed in Great Britain
by Amazon

56285936R00142